"I enthusiastically recommend that parents, businessmen, and even children read this book because it contains the knowledge, wisdom, and experience of a godly man."
Ronald W. Blue
Managing Partner, Ronald Blue & Co.

"The story of Truett Cathy's life is a story of faith, compassion, hard work, and true entrepeneurial spirit. This book can inspire others with Mr. Cathy's generosity and good works which complement his deep faith in God."
Gloria Shatto
President, Berry College

"To know Truett Cathy is to understand what being a good business person is all about. Building on basics and committed to doing proper things properly, Cathy's highly successful Chick-fil-A effectively indicates that nice folks really can be winners."
Michael H. Mescon
Dean, College of Business Administration,
Georgia State University

"Truett Cathy's *It's Easier to Succeed Than to Fail* is a book that belongs on the 'must read' list of every Christian business person. . . . I know Truett Cathy and have always admired him as a self-made man. Now I realize this is not quite the case—he is first, last, and always a God-made man."
W. Clement Stone
PMA Communications

"Mr. Cathy knows people, Scripture, and chicken. And his book, *It's Easier to Succeed Than to Fail,* has some great recipes on how to successfully mix those secret ingredients in all walks of life."
Marabel Morgan
Author

"I thoroughly enjoyed the book. Truett Cathy's life is an inspiration to anyone who believes in the free enterprise system and what you can accomplish if you are willing to work and persevere and be sure of your goals."
Carl E. Sanders
Attorney at Law

"I have admired [Truett's] entrepreneurial spirit, his Christian conviction, and his restaurant business for several years. His book exemplifies the . . . Christian Spirit."

Andrew Young
Mayor, City of Atlanta

"[Truett Cathy's] story is a splendid example for the many young people he has assisted and serves as a reminder to all that initiative, vision, and dedication are essential ingredients to a fruitful life.

James T. Laney
President, Emory University

"Truett Cathy's life can be an inspiration to any citizen anywhere in any country who wants to know if hard work, perseverance, and faith in a better future can pay off."

Newt Gingrich
U.S. Representative, Sixth District, Georgia

"Truett Cathy has proven that it is possible to build a highly successful business by putting people before profit and by seeking to honor God above pleasing men."

Pat Robertson
President, The Christian Broadcasting Network, Inc.

"A real-life case history showing that a determined and energetic entrepreneur can overcome anything. A very good read."

Philip B. Crosby
Chairman and Creative Director,
Philip Crosby Associates, Inc.

"[Truett Cathy's] influence in the life of so many young men . . . is heart warming . . . . My son Ritchie is one he has encouraged. I enthusiastically endorse this book."

Bobby Richardson
Baseball Coach, Liberty University

"[Truett Cathy's] strong Christian commitment shows clearly in every business decision that he has made. I commend the book. It will make you glad to be in a world with people like Truett Cathy."

William L. Self
Pastor, Atlanta

"A real-life story of the perfect blend of Christian principles and American entrepreneurship."

Harry S. Downs
President, Clayton State College

"The most compelling theme of Truett's story is that success is a spiritual journey before it is a corporate achievement. There is a consistency of management style . . . that pervades every decision and action."

R. Kirby Godsey
President, Mercer University

"Here is a man who has lived out his convictions. He is a true modern-day role model and hero."

Joe Edwards
Chairman of the Board,
Christopher Edwards Companies, Inc.

"[Truett Cathy] has made Christian principles and values synonymous with Chick-fil-A . . . . His story is fascinating and inspiring."

George Busbee
King & Spalding

"S. Truett Cathy inspires all of us to a higher call than what can simply be measured by the standards of this world . . . . What an encouragement and challenge for all of us!"

Sandi Patti

"Reading *It's Easier to Succeed Than to Fail* is like having a personal conversation with Truett Cathy. It's real advice from real experience. I loved it."

John Wieland
President, John Wieland Homes

"I hope [Truett's] words will serve as a catalyst for success for scores of young men and women, just as Truett's personal relationship with me has had a profound and lasting impact on my life."

Gary Gettis
Chick-fil-A Operator, Gwinnett Place Mall

"Everyone who reads this book will have their heart warmed, their life challenged, and their faith renewed."

Charles "Tremendous" Jones
Presbyterian Life Management Services

"I have been personally blessed by this [book]."
    Norman Vincent Peale

"Fascinating . . . . [*It's Easier to Succeed Than to Fail*] is another great 'Horatio Alger' story."
    Art Linkletter

"In [this book] is a wealth of information that we all need . . . . I want to recommend this book to all, men and women, young and old."
    Mary Glynn Peeples
    Successful Stress Management

"Recommended reading for Americans, a book by Truett Cathy, who proved his point before he wrote the book."
    Paul Harvey

"Eloquent in its simplicity—profound in its directness—loving in its message—and moving in its impact . . . *It's Easier to Succeed Than to Fail* is a treasury of common sense which gives its readers real hope with solid believability by virtue of the integrity of its author, Truett Cathy."
    Zig Ziglar

IT'S EASIER TO SUCCEED THAN TO FAIL

S. TRUETT CATHY

Founder and Chairman, Chick-fil-A, Inc.,
and the Dwarf House Restaurants

A Division of Thomas Nelson Publishers
NASHVILLE

Published in Nashville, Tennessee, by Oliver-Nelson Books, a division of Thomas Nelson, Inc.

Unless otherwise noted, Scripture quotations are from THE NEW KING JAMES VERSION. Copyright © 1979, 1980, 1982, Thomas Nelson, Inc., Publishers. Scripture quotations noted KJV are from The King James Version of the Holy Bible.

Every effort has been made to contact the owners or owners' agents of copyrighted material for permission to use their material. If Oliver-Nelson has included copyrighted material without the correct copyright notice or without permission, due to error or failure to locate owners/ agents or otherwise, we apologize for the error or omission and ask that the owner or owner's agent contact Oliver-Nelson supplying appropriate information. Correct information will be included in any reprinting.

For ease of reading, the term *Chick-fil-A* is used interchangeably to refer to Chick-fil-A, Inc., Chick-fil-A restaurants, Chick-fil-A products, and the Chick-fil-A organization.

Printed in the United States.

Library of Congress Cataloging-in-Publication Data

Cathy, S. Truett.
   It's easier to succeed than to fail / S. Truett Cathy.
     p. cm.
   ISBN 0-8407-9030-9
   1. Cathy, S. Truett. 2. Businessmen—United States—Biography.
  3. Chick-Fil-A Corporation—History 4. Fast food restaurants–
–United States—History. I. Title.
HC102.5.C36A3 1989
338.7'6164795'0924—dc19
  [B]   89-30181
                                        CIP

40 41 42 43 BVG 05 04 03 02

*To the thousands
of young people
who serve God
by serving our customers*

*Profits from this book
will go toward the support
of the WinShape Centre
programs.*

CONTENTS

ACKNOWLEDGMENTS

I am grateful to the Reverend Cecil Murphey and Norman B. Rohrer for their editorial counsel and many hours of assistance in the development of my book. Their efforts have helped me to share the principles by which I live and to express the appreciation I feel for my partners in the ministry of serving both physical bread and the Bread of Life.

PREFACE

"Some books are to be tasted, others to be swallowed, and some to be chewed and digested," wrote Sir Francis Bacon long ago. This book, if "chewed and digested," holds some happy surprises for people who want to enjoy God's grand design for success.

A reporter once called me for an interview. "Tell me about Truett Cathy," she began. "What I've heard sounds too good to be true!"

Ironically, Truett's thirteen-year-old boys' Sunday school class had just presented him with a plaque, which listed all their names under the bold inscription:

In Appreciation To
"True" Cathy
A Great Teacher and Friend

"Yes," I replied, "he is truly remarkable."

Truett Cathy is a very practical man who is a good steward of all the time, talents, and material resources that God has entrusted to him. Although he is dedicated to his family, faithful to his church, and committed to his business, he finds time to serve as trustee of Mercer University, Clayton State College Foundation, and the

Lord's Day Alliance of the U.S., and he is also a member of the Baptist World Alliance. Additionally, he is a member of the Rotary Club and of the First Baptist Church of Jonesboro, Georgia, where he has taught thirteen-year-old boys for many years.

Like few men I have known, Truett mirrors the apostle Paul's portrait of Christian life and service: "Not slothful in business; fervent in spirit; serving the Lord" (Rom. 12:11 KJV). He has achieved a good balance in life, and he exemplifies the proper tough-tender combination. As a highly successful businessman, he knows how and when to be tough, but the toughness is always seasoned with genuine compassion.

In his "Psalm of Life," Longfellow wrote so beautifully,

> Lives of great men all remind us
> We can make our lives sublime.
> And, departing, leave behind us
> Footprints on the sands of time.

As you read this book, you will discover that Truett Cathy has left an indelible imprint on hundreds of lives. Doubtless, your own life will be touched by his story, and this book will likely inspire thousands of others to make positive footprints on their own time and on future generations.

Enjoy a really good book as you explore Truett Cathy's credo: It's easier to succeed than to fail!

CHARLES Q. CARTER
First Baptist Church
Jonesboro, Georgia

FOREWORD

Truett Cathy has drawn from his personal experiences to write a warm and wonderfully touching guide for living. *It's Easier to Succeed Than to Fail* is a record of how growing up in the hard times of the depression and World War II formed the basis of his rules for winning.

Well-known and respected as a businessman who stands up for his principles and practices his faith daily, Mr. Cathy provides down-to-earth, practical advice for dealing with adversity. He writes of how faith can renew life, how crisis can be opportunity in disguise, and how every problem can have a solution.

The phenomenal success of Chick-fil-A is solid evidence that winning is a way of life for Truett Cathy.

DONALD R. KEOUGH
President and Chief Operating Officer
The Coca-Cola Company

INTRODUCTION

One bright morning in June, I told the graduating students of Clayton State College in Morrow, Georgia, at their commencement exercises that "it's easier to succeed than to fail."

A fellow who had been in the audience wrote to me several weeks later from Europe where he was traveling: "Your words are still ringing in my ears but I can't figure out what you mean by, 'It's easier to succeed than to fail.' Maybe some day I'll be old enough to understand."

Well, the answer is quite simple. It's the theme of this book, and I hope it will help you to succeed in ways you might otherwise have missed.

- It's easier to succeed because *failure exacts a high price in terms of time when you have to do a job over.*
- It's easier to succeed because *success eliminates the agony and frustration of defeat.*
- It's easier to succeed because *money spent to fail must be spent again to succeed.*
- It's easier to succeed because *a person's credibility decreases with each failure, making it harder to succeed the second time.*

- And it's easier to succeed because *joy and expressions of affirmation come from succeeding, whereas feelings of discouragement and discontent accompany failure.*

A highly successful person was asked, "How did you become successful?"

He replied, "By making the right decisions."

"How did you know which decisions to make?" was the next question.

"By the experiences I've had."

"How did you gain experience?"

"By making bad decisions," he responded.

That man profited by his mistakes. He also profited by observing other people's mistakes and failures. This procedure is a shortcut to success.

It is important to involve God in all of our decisions. He is a supernatural resource of power and strength and wisdom that we often fail to take advantage of. We glorify God in our successes rather than in our failures.

God has built within us all a strong desire to be successful. Many times, in speaking to young people, I ask the question, "How many of you would like to be successful?" I have yet to hear the answer that they want to be flops.

But the conduct and attitudes of many young people and adults make it seem as though they purposefully do things that hinder them from being successful. Some people detest "work," but all enjoy "accomplishments."

Are you willing to make temporary sacrifices to receive greater dividends in the future?

I have learned through more than forty years of

business experience these three keys to success that work for all people under every circumstance:

1. You have to *want* to succeed. You have to be willing to make a generous commitment of time and energy. When I went into the restaurant business, I lived next door to the place I called the Dwarf House. When I wasn't on the job, I went back to my room to catch a few hours of sleep. One time I worked thirty-six hours at a stretch without even sitting down.

2. You have to develop *know-how*. Merely putting time and energy into a project isn't enough. You have to study your projected market. You have to develop skills. Prepare yourself physically, mentally, and intellectually through formal education.

3. Finally, you have to *do* it. Some people prepare themselves by getting a fine education; they come from a good home; they have the right opportunities, but they blow them because they don't put into action what they have learned.

Everyone has a built-in success formula. God wants you to succeed, but let the obstacles come from Him, not from you. Don't disobey His laws and put obstacles in His way.

There's always a better way. This book is dedicated to helping you find it.

1

HERE'S TO THE WINNERS

*N*ot even God can change the past, but He can do a lot of wonderful things about the future if we'll let Him. Each person's destiny is not a matter of chance; it's a matter of choice. It's determined by what we say, what we do, and whom we trust.

Often people ask, "Why are you so interested in young people?" My answer is that I can't think of a better segment of our society in which to invest my time and resources. It seems as if all of my adult life I've been surrounded by kids. My wife and I reared three of our own children, who gave us ten grandchildren; we have opened our home to several foster children as well; we employ more than fifteen thousand young people in various Chick-fil-A restaurant Units; I've taught thirteen-year-old boys in Sunday school for thirty years and currently enjoy teaching a class of more than thirty boys at the First Baptist Church of Jonesboro, Georgia.

Our family foundation funds our own college campus, which we call WinShape Centre ("Shaping individuals to be winners"). It has attracted more than four hundred college students who live on our campus and commute to the main campus of Berry College three miles away. These students are on a four-year $10,000 tuition scholarship: $5,000 provided by Berry College and $5,000 by the foundation.

We also have boys' camps in the summer, two-week sessions spread over an eight-week period. We started our first camping session in 1985 with 255 boys and steadily increased to 472 boys by 1988. During the past four years, we have registered approximately 1,550 boys. The theme for our boys' camps is: "It's Better To Build Boys Than To Mend Men." In 1987, we organized a girls' camp three miles away, which attracted 116 at the beginning camp. The response was exactly double the following year when 232 girls attended our camp.

In addition to these camps, the WinShape Centre Foundation sponsors a foster home, which has full-time paid parents. Ten boys and two girls currently live in that home. They are not troublemakers. They have no emotional or behavioral problems. Conditions at home might be against them, but they still want to make winners out of themselves. Our strategy is to attract those individuals we can encourage to do their best so that they can get through college and make something of their lives. Even though many of these children have parents who are delinquent in their responsibilities, the kids want to rise above their environment. Two additional foster homes are being planned for 1989, a second home at WinShape Centre and one in Atlanta in South Fulton County, and we plan to further expand our foster care program.

For more than three decades, our farm has been the gathering place of a steady stream of young people. Along with my Sunday school class and the winners of $1,000 scholarships offered by our Chick-fil-A restaurants nationwide have come fatherless boys, runaways,

* ─────────────────

*To succeed,
try this suggestion
for success:
save 10 percent,
give 10 percent,
work 10 percent
harder.*

─────────────────

candidates for the Paul Anderson Youth Home, boys from Christian City in College Park, Georgia, students from Berry College, friends of our own children, and youngsters from broken homes who have trouble fitting in.

In some cases, I probably have been the first adult to show love and a willingness to listen to their problems. We've spent time together on my farm, riding dirt bikes and horses, talking, eating, listening, looking at the world from an adult's perspective, and learning lessons from the Bible.

Each year I ask the new group of boys in my Sunday school class what they would change in their homes if they could. Most of them say, "I would stop the arguing at home." The best gift a mother and a dad can give to their children is to love each other and live under the same roof. Everything else is of lesser importance.

May I introduce my friend Hal? At sixteen, he was working part-time at a Chick-fil-A Unit while attending high school. One day his mother phoned me to say that Hal was especially discouraged in school and not happy on the job. His father was deceased, and the boy needed a male image at this critical stage of life.

"In a few hours I'll be flying to North Carolina for the grand opening of a new Chick-fil-A restaurant," I told Hal's mother. "Do you think Hal would like to go with me?"

"It would mean skipping school on Friday," she replied, "but I don't think Hal will mind that one bit."

Hal and I discussed many things on that trip. On the way back, I offered him this recipe for being happy and successful: *Select those jobs that others dislike.*

"When you report for work," I suggested, "see if you can get the assignment of keeping the rest rooms clean. (He thought he probably could get that job!) This time, clean the walls and the floors with extra effort. Shine those mirrors. And when you get to the commode, clean it as though you're going to drink out of it. And after you've done your best, better than anyone else has ever done it, step back and receive the thrill of a job well done."

Hal's smile told me he was ready to give it a try. There is a lot of Scripture to support the statement that we honor God and God honors us when we perform at our best in *everything* we do. Only then can we realize our greatest potential.

One autumn my wife and I invited to our house for Thanksgiving a group of seven orphaned boys from Gainesville, Georgia. They were brothers, ranging in age from eight to nineteen, trying desperately to stay together after their father abandoned the home and their mother died of a brain tumor at the age of thirty-one.

The boys' grandfather came to live with them, but before many months passed, he also died. After bouncing around from one job to another and from one residence to another, their father showed up briefly to claim the tractor and a truck. He sold the chicken houses and made off with other valuables, leaving his sons $32,000 in debt.

The eldest son took charge. He had promised his dying mother that he would "keep the boys together." Like a drill sergeant, he gave orders, and gradually the seven brothers were able to make their own way. The $400 carned each week from outside jobs could take care of current expenses but not the heavy indebtedness that hung over them.

The Department of Family and Children Services assigned the four youngest boys to other quarters, but the eldest fought to get them back.

After hearing of their problems, I asked him, "Why don't you just do your own thing?"

"Well," he said (as I expected he would), "my thing is to take care of my brothers."

We enjoyed having them in our home, and they enjoyed getting away from the pressures of their chicken farm for the holidays. They're a lovable group of boys. No two of them are alike. If all of the national attention doesn't corrupt them, they'll be fine. I've been to their chicken farm several times and will continue to keep in touch with these potential winners.

On another occasion, my wife and I invited to our house for a few weeks a young fellow from a home with many troubles. His parents were unstable, and his brothers and sisters did not hold down honorable jobs. But Allen was different. I said to him one day, "Allen, here's ten dollars so you'll have some spending money."

"No, sir," he replied. "I can't take money from people unless I earn it."

"Well," I explained, "this is just a little gift. I want you to have it for pocket change."

"No," he repeated, "I wouldn't be able to take it."

A young man at Furman University approached me one day and asked if he could work for Chick-fil-A.

"What are some of the things you like to do?" I asked him.

"Well," he said, "I've had three different jobs, and

I've been successful at them all—house painting, waiting tables, and carpentry."

That young man had lots of options open to him. He selected a career in Chick-fil-A and has done an outstanding job.

So did Wayne at that age. He was in my Sunday school class at the age of thirteen. We were talking one Lord's Day about habits, good and bad. The subject of cigarette smoking came up. Wayne said he had never smoked.

"Really, Wayne?" I exclaimed, knowing the temptations of thirteen-year-old boys, and knowing also that his mother and father smoked so there were plenty of cigarettes around the house. "How is it that you *never* smoked?"

"When I was nine years old and my sister was thirteen, we made a vow that we would never put a cigarette to our lips, and we have kept that vow to this day."

Years later, Wayne came into my office. "Mr. Cathy," he began, "I'd like to talk to you about operating one of your restaurants."

My first question was, "Did you smoke that first cigarette yet?"

He shook his head. "No, sir, I haven't."

"Let's sit down and talk," I said.

Some people might ask, "Is it all that important that Wayne didn't smoke a cigarette?" Maybe not to some people. But to me, it showed that Wayne lived a disciplined life, that he honored a vow, and that he wanted to do the things that were good for him without letting others dictate what he would and would not do. Today, Wayne operates one of our top three restaurants. He has a beautiful wife and two fine youngsters. With the gratification which success in business has brought him, he also enjoys trail bikes, motorcycles, boats, show horses, and recreational vehicles down on his farm. Principles that are observed in youth carry over into adulthood.

Each restaurant Operator who attended our annual seminar in 1985 received a plaque that read:

Associate yourselves only with those people
you can be proud of
whether they work for you or you work for them.

I tell the boys in my Sunday school class, "If you want to be an *A* student, associate with *A* students; if you want to be an athlete, associate with athletes; if you want to be a winner in anything, associate with people who are winners." Then I often add with a smile, "If you want to be bald, associate with baldheaded people . . . like me."

My friend Charles "Tremendous" Jones ends every speech with this statement: "You'll be the same person five years from now as you are today except for the books you read and the people you associate yourself with." I agree. I hope I'm not the same person today that I was five years ago.

An Operator said to me one day in my office, "Truett, you can't possibly relate to us out there in the Chick-fil-A Units. We're in crowded conditions, with noise and confusion. . . . Here you sit in this nice quiet office with lots of space."

"How long have you been in business?" I asked.

"Four years."

"Do you know how long I've been in the restaurant

business? For more than *forty* years. It's how you handle problems that makes the difference, not whether you have problems."

When I was in grammar school, the teacher would select from the homeroom a Scripture reference for the week. One morning my verse, chosen with the help of my mother, was the week's verse: "A good name is rather to be chosen than great riches" (Prov. 22:1 KJV). That made an impression on me. Making correct choices is the way to build a reputation and the way to learn how to handle problems.

A decade or so ago Terry, the young son of a pastor, asked me to lend him $500 for a car.

"What are you doing these days?" I asked him.

"I'm working at the bank."

"You mean they let you work at the bank with that long hair?"

"Yeah, I work in the stockroom. If I get promoted and work at the counter, I'll get my hair cut."

"Tell you what," I proposed. "I'll honor your request for a loan if you'll get your hair cut."

He said, "Well, Mr. Cathy, you're judging me on the outside for what I am on the inside."

"That's true," I acknowledged, "but I can't see you on the inside. I can only see you on the outside, and I have come to some conclusions about what I'm able to see."

I continued, "I know a girl who is five feet tall and five feet wide, snaggletoothed, bowlegged, and bald-headed. Would you date her?"

"I guess I wouldn't," Terry admitted.

"Well, you're doing the same thing you're accusing me of doing, judging a person on the inside by what you see on the outside. You haven't even given her a chance."

The young man got the haircut, but sadly I had not specified how short. Although his haircut wasn't what I had intended, he got his loan for the car. Today Terry Quick is the pastor of a successful church in our community.

It's worthy of note that we behave as we dress. If we dress in our good clothes and shine our shoes, we will be more careful about how we act. In our Chick-fil-A restaurants, I stress the need for neat, clean clothing. Customers can choose from many places to eat. They are quick to pick the most appealing restaurant, and the appearance of the people who work in it can affect such decisions favorably or unfavorably.

A good attitude is one of the best guarantees of success. A less-qualified individual with a good attitude would be more welcomed at my company than a highly talented individual with a bad attitude. A successful baseball coach once said that if you have a player on your team who is skillful but has a bad attitude, the sooner you get rid of that person, the better the team will be.

I found this to be true among our Chick-fil-A Operators, too. Sometimes we've been guilty of being too lenient toward people, too slow to make a change.

We once sent an Operator $3,000 from company funds for advertising. One of our home staff members sat down with him to discuss his ad program.

"Well," he snapped, "if you're going to tell me how to spend this money, you can just take it back."

One day a girl was washing dishes in my restaurant, complaining all the time. "Here," said a coworker, "you bread chicken for a while, and I'll wash those dishes."

"Oh, no!" the girl replied. "I don't like to bread chicken either."

My young friend Eddie White, on the other hand, always worked joyfully and seemed to look for a way to do just a little more than anyone asked of him at the original Dwarf House restaurant. He came to work for me at the age of twelve, before we had child labor laws in Georgia. Eddie, active in his church, is an outstanding Christian.

Eddie's goal was to be a medical missionary. After his high-school graduation, he passed up a college scholarship because his father told him he would have to work full-time and help support the rest of the children until they graduated from high school. Being an obedient child, Eddie respected what his father said and postponed his schooling.

I went to his house one afternoon and asked his father to reconsider his decision. At length, Mr. White said he would allow Eddie to enroll in college, provided the boy continued to work and to give half his earnings toward the support of the family.

Eddie agreed without hesitating. However, when he applied, he discovered that the scholarship had gone to someone else. But that didn't hinder him from enrolling.

One of the waitresses at the Dwarf House placed a gallon jar near the cash register so that customers could contribute to the Scholarship Fund for Eddie White. When it was time for Eddie to enter college, the funds collected weren't enough, so it was my privilege to make up the difference. I invited him to continue working at my restaurant. I didn't give the money as a handout.

Eddie sometimes worked as many as sixty hours a week during vacation periods. He once said, "Mr. Cathy, the Whites are a proud family. My father doesn't want me to learn to take handouts."

In 1984 I established a scholarship fund in Eddie's name at his alma mater, Morris Brown College, a predominantly black college in Atlanta. Others plan to add to the fund, and in time, the interest alone can be used for scholarship aid.

Because of the expense of training in medicine, Eddie changed to a major in education. It was a hard decision to make, but once he made it, Eddie never looked back with regret.

It would take many pages to tell about all of Eddie's activities and achievements. He has taught for twenty-three years in the Clayton County school system, and he is the principal of a junior high school in Clayton County, Georgia. Eddie has received the Outstanding Educator Award from the Forest Park Jaycees and a Citizenship Award from the College Park Civic/ Education Club. For two consecutive years, he received the prestigious STAR Teacher Award from the Forest Park Senior High School. He has gotten involved in everything from the Red Cross to a countywide beautification project. He is part of the Sheriff's Department Protection of Youth and is a PTA council member. Eddie serves as a deacon and a Sunday school teacher at Atlanta's Traveler's Rest Baptist Church, and he has helped to organize a new church pastored by his brother, Henry.

Recently, Eddie said some of the most touching

words to me I've ever heard, "I looked for acceptance in the adult world, and you accepted me as part of your family. I can never forget that."

I'll end this chapter with the story of a fine-looking, curly haired boy who increased his spiritual vision from zero to twenty-twenty within only a few months. Jeannette and I first met him at the Atlanta airport in 1978 while we were waiting to board a plane for Boston. He was standing behind us in a line to receive his seat assignment. I noticed that the woman with him held only one ticket and that the boy was blind.

"Excuse me," I said to the woman, "is the boy traveling alone?"

"Why, yes, he is," she replied.

"Could we be of service?"

"Would you?" I saw the relief on her face.

The fourteen-year-old boy, Gene Hubbard, was also deaf and mute. The woman instructed me how to interpret two hand signals—one to notify us that he wanted to go to the bathroom, the other to express his friendship. Gene was enrolled in the Perkins School for the Blind in Boston where someone from that school was scheduled to meet him at the plane.

Gene kept me busy during the flight. First, he wanted his tray in front of his seat. Since we sat in the front row of the tourist section, I had to insert the tray in the proper holes. He had brought along candy and cookies. After eating his snacks, Gene wanted a drink. Then he needed a straw. How amazing it was that he could relate his needs to others without words. When the flight attendants served the meal, we helped him eat. He had to go to the bathroom three times during the flight.

The representative from Perkins in Boston knew little about Gene, but she put me in touch with his caseworker in South Carolina, who gave me the full story of this young man:

Before he was a year old, Gene had become a ward of the court. An early childhood illness had left him blind, deaf, and unable to speak. Since no one wanted to adopt him, the state sent him to a school for the blind in Talladega, Alabama.

Through a woman named Thelma Lewis, who knew Gene as a close friend, I began writing to Gene. He answered in braille, but the staff at Perkins kindly added the translation so that I could read Gene's letters. I sent him Chick-fil-A T-shirts occasionally, and he always wrote back to thank me.

One Christmas, Gene sent me a piece of pottery molded by his own hands, with his name printed on the bottom. I still keep this treasure on my desk at home as a reminder of Gene. If I ever feel sorry for myself, I turn my thoughts to that courageous boy.

One day the caseworker wrote me a crushing letter. She explained in detail that Gene had been having severe pain in his left leg. An examination indicated cancer, and the doctors had to amputate his left leg. Tears stung my eyes when I read the most painful words of all: "They expect him to live only about six more months."

I wept and cried out to God, "How can this be? I know You are a merciful God, but with all the problems that boy has had in his life, how can You let this happen to him?"

Despite all his handicaps, that boy brought pleasure to people around him. He had a warm smile and a bit of humor in some of the things he did. Above all, he was lovable.

Mrs. Lewis earnestly wanted Gene to visit her one last time. She also requested that, after his death, his body be buried next to her son, who had been partially blind.

I helped with part of the expense of sending him back for a visit with Mrs. Lewis in Talladega. When Gene was en route back to Boston, she brought him by my office in Atlanta. Gene sat in a wheelchair, weakened by cancer and by the amputation of his leg. "He suffers a lot of pain," Mrs. Lewis explained, "because the doctors and nurses can't always determine how much or where he hurts."

As predicted, Gene died within six months. The Perkins School for the Blind shipped his body to Mrs. Lewis. Two young people who had worked with Gene during the last months of his illness escorted the casket. The Talladega School for the Blind held a special service for Gene. The place was filled with teachers and students who were blind and/or deaf. I served as a pallbearer. At the funeral, and later when I talked with people, I realized how many lives Gene Hubbard had touched in the sixteen years of life.

"Do you think Gene ever understood enough to have a relationship with God?" I asked.

"Yes, I do," Mrs. Lewis said. "When I think about his contentment, his cooperative spirit, and the positive influence he had on others, I have to believe that he was sensitive to God's direction in his life.

"One day he was holding a butterfly that had died

in a jar. I watched him carry it outside and toss it up into the air. And in *his* way of communicating, he was saying, 'Gone to be with God.' "

As I wiped away my own tears, I thought, *God must have a special, special place for people like Gene.* I thank God for the opportunity to have known him.

Here's to the winners, for they give each task their best effort and find in the end that it's easier to succeed than to fail.

What shall you give to one small boy?
A glamorous game, a tinseled toy,
A fancy knife, a puzzle pack,
A train that runs on a curving track,
A picture book, a real live pet?

No! There's plenty of time for such things yet.
Give him a day for his very own.
Just one small boy and his dad alone.
A walk in the woods, a romp in the park,
A fishing trip from dawn to dark.

Give him the finest gift you can—
The companionship of a grownup man.
Games are outgrown, and toys decay,
But he'll never forget the gift of a day!*

Vital Christianity, August 1, 1976.

2

YOU CAN'T SUCCEED
IF YOU DON'T START

The longest journey begins with the first step. Ahead of each person is a pilgrimage to success, a journey characterized by challenge and adventure.

A person cannot live without goals. God put within each of us the quest for success. If He had not, we would still be cooking over an open fire. As Solomon said, "It is the glory of God to conceal a matter, but the glory of kings is to search out a matter" (Prov. 25:2).

In Tyler, Texas, a boy still in his teens walked into a grocery store where some men were sitting around a stove. "Say, sonny, what are you going to be when you grow up?" one of them asked with a broad grin.

"I'll tell you what I'm going to be," the boy answered. "I'm going to be the best lawyer in the world—that's what I'm going to be if you want to know."

The loafers laughed heartily as the boy picked up his groceries and left quietly. Later that boy, Martin W. Littleton, became a recognized authority in the legal world.

A young salesman in a hardware store once observed an accumulation of odds and ends that were out of date and not selling. He rigged up a special table, marked the items at a dime each, and cleaned them out fast. F. W. Woolworth made a fortune through his five-and-dime stores.

A. L. Williams was a high school football coach who decided to supplement his $10,700 salary by selling term life insurance. He found he could help other families avoid the financial crisis his mother faced when his father died unexpectedly. Williams believed not only in what he was doing, but also in himself. He quit coaching and in 1977 started his own company on the buy-term-and-invest-the-difference concept. Today that company is an industry leader and Williams is a multimillionaire.

On a wall in my office hangs a reproduction of a poster that my daughter Trudy sent from summer camp a few years ago. It reads, "No goal is too high if we climb with care and confidence."

Sometimes a person becomes too aggressive in the pursuit of business and overextends himself. Activity does not guarantee success. Activity must be matched with competence. Sometimes it is better to do less and do it with contentment than to do more and be exhausted.

Sometimes we do things right, and nothing happens. But if we're not careful, we give up just at the goal line instead of going ahead and eventually accomplishing the goals that we have set.

Life is not easy, but it's exciting, fun, and rewarding. The most exciting thing is that you can choose to do with it what you will.

My life began early in the Roaring Twenties. I arrived with the boll weevil in Putnam County, Georgia, where Joel Chandler Harris had written his famous Un-

*⟶

*We glorify God
in our successes
rather than
in our failures.*

cle Remus stories a generation earlier. The classic stories of Br'er Rabbit who always outwitted Br'er Fox were first published in Eatonton, my birthplace.

When I was four, my parents, Joseph Benjamin and Lilla Kimbell Cathy, moved to Atlanta, which became home for my four sisters and two brothers and me. My parents had their hands full with Esther, Agnes, Myrtle, Horace, Gladys, me, and Ben. In Atlanta I chose my three *M*'s: mission, mate, and master. At the age of eight, I went into the business of serving Cokes, and so my *mission* was born; at the same age in 1929, I met my *mate*, although I didn't court her until a decade and a half later. When I was twelve, I received Christ as my personal Savior and thus decided who my *Master* would be.

After the stock market crash of 1929, property dropped to nearly zero, taking my father's real estate business with it. My mother opened our home to boarders, and my father established a rural insurance route for the Life and Casualty Company. His was a debit route on which he collected on life and accidental death policies that yielded sometimes only nickels and dimes. Dad worked hard, but he could not make an adequate living for his large family. Often he would bring home in his Model T sorghum syrup, chicken, country hams, and other goods from policyholders too poor to pay their premiums in cash.

Mother worked like a slave, keeping house and cooking for her seven children and a houseful of boarders. I never saw her eyes closed in sleep. Not until she lay in her coffin did I see my saintly mother at rest. On Sunday afternoon she would play the piano and sing the old hymns. She tuned faithfully to hear Charles E.

Fuller preach on "The Old Fashioned Revival Hour" from Long Beach, California.

Dad never recovered from the depression. He could not rise above discouragement, relied heavily on the older children to take care of him, and verbally abused my mother, who was criticized if she answered and criticized if she didn't.

Growing up in a boarding house introduced me to hard work and taught me the value of diligent labor. I learned to shuck corn, shell peas, wash dirty dishes, set the table, shop for my mother at the corner grocery store, and even flip eggs and pancakes on the grill.

I was named Samuel after a pastor friend of my parents and Truett after the great Southern Baptist pastor George W. Truett, longtime pastor of First Baptist Church in Dallas, Texas. As a youngster, I was tongue-tied and couldn't pronounce certain sounds. At school, about the best I could do in pronouncing my name was "ooit-a-ee." Mother would send along my name on a card for each new teacher. Public speaking came late in my adult life, only after I taught my Sunday school class for several decades and later when asked to address associates in the business community.

When I was in the second grade, I noticed one day while I was running errands all over Atlanta's West End that I could buy Coca-Cola in bottles six for a quarter. I peddled them to our neighbors for five cents each and made a nickel profit. When I sold out, I'd run back to Rogers Grocery Store on the corner of Oak and Ashby streets and buy more.

"Truett," a neighbor told me one day, "if you'd ice these Cokes down, we'd buy more."

I "borrowed" chips of ice from Mother's icebox and coaxed some off the iceman's truck as it rumbled down Oak Street. The Coca-Cola truck also traveled that street, so I began to flag him down to buy a case of twenty-four cokes for eighty cents. This gave me a profit of forty cents if I didn't have to buy any ice. Even if I did, ice cost only eight cents for twenty-five pounds.

At a refreshment stand in our front yard, I added Orange Crush and Nu Grape to my menu. Business picked up.

When the weather turned cold, I peddled magazines from door to door. *The Ladies' Home Journal* sold for ten cents, so I enjoyed a profit of four cents. For *The Saturday Evening Post,* I charged five cents and made a profit of a penny and a half. You can guess which magazine I tried to sell first. If a customer couldn't buy the ten-cent magazine, I'd pull out the five-cent periodical. A cent and a half was better than nothing. I always thought the rich bought the ten-cent magazine and the poor bought the one that cost five cents. I didn't think the contents were all that important.

When I was eleven years old, I began helping a newspaper boy distribute his papers in the dawn's early light. He often gave me full responsibilities for putting the papers at the right houses and at the right place "behind the screen door, out of the rain, and away from the dog."

At the age of twelve, I got my own route for the *Atlanta Journal.* From the election of Franklin D. Roosevelt in 1933 until Pearl Harbor in 1941, I threw the news—good and bad—on the doorsteps of customers. That was my daily job all those years during my boyhood. I made my rounds in the evening on week days and early in the morning on Sundays.

Most of the young fellows who dragged out before dawn had their fathers' help with the family car in rainy or cold weather. Not me. Father would stay in bed, having not the least inclination to yield to my pleading for his help or for the use of the family automobile, no matter how severe the weather.

Gradually, my resources rose to the tidy sum of four dollars, and I was able to buy a neighbor's bicycle. It had two round wheels and a frame; that was about it. The purchase was a significant undertaking in my life, though, and I was proud of it.

A neighbor who also attended Joe Brown Junior High School and the West End Baptist Church was a girl named Jeannette McNeil. I met her at the age of eight and secretly admired her very much. She later moved away, and I lost track of the person who would one day become my wife.

After my high school graduation, World War II and the Selective Service interrupted my budding enterprises. My brother Ben and I were drafted into the U.S. Army. God makes us into the persons He intends as we become obedient in the small details of life. I was ready to lay aside my own youthful endeavors and have my faith tested in the world of military service.

Ben was younger than I, but he was drafted first because I was working for the Civil Service at Atlanta's General Depot, now called Fort Gillem. I became the administrative assistant on a traveling crew that repaired equipment and vehicles vital to the war effort. I gave the job my best efforts and enjoyed traveling with the crew and living in government barracks. Two hundred mechanics in three groupings worked under my supervision. I reported directly to Major Frederick Spencer.

Major Joseph Haas, my friend and the adjutant for the post, on two occasions succeeded in having me deferred, but eventually the draft board called me up. Major Haas assigned me to the Atlanta General Depot so that I could do the same kind of work I had been doing as a civilian, but with less pay, of course.

Probably no one else in the United States Army received my style of basic military training. I was a platoon of *one*. Master Sergeant Banks taught me personally the various drills, steps, and commands. Frankly, it was embarrassing to march alone beside Sergeant Banks as he called cadence. Friends who did not understand my situation thought I was being punished.

While I was serving as a clerk with military personnel, updating records and keeping awards and medals information in order, Ben was in northern Europe fighting without adequate clothing or food. He almost lost his toes because of frostbite. Later, he fought with a unit in Italy that had 80 percent casualties.

In 1944, the army transferred me to Fort Lewis, Washington. My entire ordnance unit was scheduled to be sent to fight in the South Pacific.

Warm weather made sunbathing delightful as we waited for our orders, but I developed a curious allergy to sunlight. My skin felt as though it was being stretched every time I took off my shirt. My head ached, and I would black out.

"Probably a mild case of sunstroke," a doctor in

the dispensary decided. "You haven't been used to the sun lately."

When my company finally shipped out, the doctors kept me behind and tried to find a way to help me so that I could join another unit. But they found no solution.

"We're releasing you so you can return to duty," a doctor said as he wrote out his report.

"Return to duty?" I exclaimed, unable to believe what he had said. "I can't go overseas like this! I certainly can't go to the South Pacific."

He shrugged. "We can't do anything more for you. We have to send you back to duty."

"But I won't be any good in the Pacific," I insisted. "The first time I take off a shirt in that broiling heat I'm done for."

"Hmmm. Well, I'll think about it and let you know," the doctor replied.

I heard nothing for two weeks. I didn't want to shirk my duty, but I wasn't eager to rush into combat if I was in danger of blacking out every time I got too much sun.

At the end of the two weeks, I received my discharge and train fare back to Georgia. "Cathy," one doctor said, "you'll have to learn to live with it. We've done all we know to help you."

I lived with my curious malady until one day I decided to experiment. Unless I exposed to the sunlight some part of my body that was normally covered, I was okay. For exactly ten seconds, I exposed my arms, then quickly covered them up—just enough exposure so my skin felt it but not enough for a reaction. I did that every day for several weeks, then increased my exposure to fifteen seconds and allowed the sun to strike my legs as well. By following that procedure and gradually increasing the times, in two years all allergic reactions had vanished, never to return.

Both Ben and I were discharged in 1945. I was twenty-three, and Ben was almost twenty-one. We had talked vaguely about going into business together, but what type? I thought about a grocery store (long before the nationwide supermarket chains took over) and/or the restaurant business.

The decision settled itself when Price Morton, a friend of my sister Gladys, talked to me. Price managed the Dutch Kitchen Restaurant. The owner, Mrs. Susan Brownlee (not her real name), was shrewd enough to make the place pay, and she had plans to expand into a chain of restaurants around Atlanta. Mrs. Brownlee hired us for a training period, promising that Ben and I would both have a restaurant to manage after that.

For seven weeks, we worked twelve hours a day, seven days a week, in Mrs. Brownlee's Dutch Kitchen, but she would not live up to her agreement to give us each a restaurant to manage. She suggested we manage one together, so we quit and made plans to start our own restaurant.

For the eating place I envisioned, I needed Ben. The restaurant would stay open twenty-four hours a day. That would mean twelve-hour shifts for each of us. We would cook everything on the grill, so our menu would be limited to things such as hamburgers and french fries, small steaks, and a typical breakfast menu.

We would need approximately $10,000 to open. From the sale of my car and our pooled savings, we accumulated nearly $4,000. Friends advised that we borrow the rest from the bank. With the war over, the economy was trying to get back to normal. There was a boom in housing, and banks seemed eager to help people like us get started in business.

We jointly applied for $6,600 and began looking for a place to start. I'm glad I didn't know the problems we would face. Had I known, I probably wouldn't have had the determination to start.

We looked at closed-down restaurants and didn't like any of them; most were in bad locations. We decided to buy a piece of property. "We'll design our own building," I said, even though neither of us had ever done anything like that before.

The Ford Motor Company broke ground for an assembly plant in Hapeville on the south side of Atlanta at about the time we located a desirable piece of property nearby. Although not a corner lot, it was next to the corner on a site that gave us a good traffic flow. Industry was moving to that area. I knew we had a chance to work up a good breakfast trade with people going to work, and we could develop a good lunch trade as well.

The die was cast. We were on our way. Difficulties lay ahead, but we believed that many miracles are performed by hard work and that we would succeed only if we made a start.

3

THE DWARF HOUSE —A GIANT STEP

Work is fun when we are doing what we like to do and are performing at our best. Many people have never experienced job satisfaction simply because they are not performing at their greatest potential and won't give it their best shot. Many "miracles" are simply the result of hard work.

Studies show that between 65 percent and 80 percent of working people do not like what they are doing for a living. That's a sad fact because a person spends one-third of his life on the job.

Sometimes I go home in the evening dead tired. I've come to realize that it's not the things I *do* that make me tired; it's worrying about the things I *don't* get done that makes me tired. If you always do your best and leave the rest for another day, you'll feel good about your accomplishments.

The lot at 461 South Central Avenue in the Atlanta suburb of Hapeville that Ben and I bought for our restaurant measured 50 feet wide at the street and was 150 feet deep. The owner, Mrs. Hammond, agreed to sell it for $2,500. With the $4,000 from our personal resources plus $6,600 borrowed from the First National Bank of

Atlanta, we had $10,600. With that "enormous sum," we thought we could buy any part of the world.

We set a date to close the sale. The lawyer casually remarked, "You're taking care of the zoning change, I suppose."

"What zoning change?" I asked.

The shock on his face showed, even though he tried not to let it. "Why," he said, "you can't just open a restaurant there. It's zoned for residential use only. You'll have to get it changed for business use."

"How do you do that?"

He sent me to Hapeville's City Hall where I filled out a request. Then I had to appear before the zoning board and put up signs on the property announcing our intentions to rezone the property. To our relief, no one objected.

We hired a contractor who agreed to build our restaurant for cost plus 10 percent, and we put our stamp of approval on his one-page blueprint. While working for Mrs. Brownlee, I had learned some ways to make better use of space, how to install equipment better, and how to cut down on the number of steps required for waiting on customers.

Once that was settled, I turned to face bigger problems. The year was 1946, one year after World War II had ended. For five years, the country had geared production toward the war effort. Now industry was trying to catch up with the civilian demand.

"Don't expect I'll have anything to sell you for about five, maybe six months," one supplier said.

"We're starting to get building materials," another told me, "but frankly, I have to give them to the big con-

* ———————————

Learn to love your work, and you'll never have to "work" again.

———————————

tractors. They're the ones who keep me in business. Sorry."

I couldn't wait for five or six months. Ben and I had to get that building up so we could start earning a living. I went everywhere picking up and bargaining for used materials. When I found usable wood from torn-down buildings, I tried to buy it, regardless of the size. For other materials like cement, I bought one bag (the limit of many stores) at one place and went to another for a second bag.

Nails were the hardest items to come by. All steel had gone into the war effort. Then I had an idea: What about buying prewar nails? To get them, I drove to outlying towns where people hadn't done much building for many years. In towns of four and five hundred people I could buy a few pounds of eightpenny or sixteen-penny nails or any size that they would sell. Between buying nails in small towns and straightening old ones, Ben and I spent a lot of hours, but we didn't keep track of the time spent. We put all our energy into getting the restaurant finished.

We didn't even try to buy new equipment. Instead, all of the equipment came from restaurants that had gone out of business. We sanded, painted, repaired, and polished everything, and we were pleased with the results.

On top of that, Ben and I did a lot of manual labor—anything to lower the costs. The two of us dug most of the footings for the building, learned to hang Sheetrock, and drove nails for most of the framing.

As the building neared completion and the day for our grand opening was set, we encountered our next problem. That obstacle, more than any other, almost kept us from opening. We couldn't buy enough food for our grill. The government still kept strict controls on meat. We couldn't go into any store and buy pork, beef, or even cooking oil in quantities we would need. To add to the problem, we couldn't get ketchup, sugar, and many other essential items for our menu.

The bigger and well-established restaurants had little trouble. They had been fighting this battle all through the war years and knew every way to buy extra sides of beef or pork. They got first choice, which left nothing for the newcomers.

One principle I've learned to believe in—and it came in handy in those days—was this: *Every problem has a solution.* That may sound pretty strong, but if we stay at a problem, keep thinking, and don't quit, one day we will find the answer. That's how it worked with the foodstuffs.

I went to Mr. Whitton, the manager of Kimball House in Atlanta. In those days it was one of the city's most fashionable restaurants, and I had known the manager for years.

"I've got a problem, and I'd sure like your help," I told him. I explained that Kimball House and the other big restaurants bought up all the meat, leaving none for us. I told him about the restaurant Ben and I were trying to get started.

Mr. Whitton was a kindhearted man. He figured out what I wanted before I even asked for it. "You'd like me to order what you need along with our supplies, is that it?"

I smiled. He understood.

"Sure. Why not?"

That was how we obtained not only meat but also

cooking oil, ketchup, and other essentials for our Dwarf Grill. Later, when business boomed, we could no longer get enough meat through Kimball House. We had to find a new source of supply or go out of business.

For several days, I mulled over the problem before I had another idea. "Ben, it seems to me we could go directly to local farmers and buy from them. What do you think?"

He was all for it. "Probably end up getting it cheaper, too," he said.

We thought of all the possible problems and figured we could work them out. The Hooks Freezer Locker Plant in Jonesboro processed beef for the farmers. We bought most of our beef there. It wasn't government inspected, but we were so desperate that we bought it anyway. Other restaurants did the same thing. We learned how to select good meat. Today we make quality a priority in our selection of chicken for our expanding restaurant chain.

Despite all the setbacks, we opened on schedule in May of 1946. I won't ever forget the day we turned on the neon sign that proclaimed "Dwarf Grill." As I looked at those red letters beaming back at us, it was the proudest moment of my life to that point. *It's our place*, I kept thinking. *We own it.* I remembered all of the obstacles we had overcome, and at times they had seemed insurmountable. But we had done it.

I walked around the outside alone, my heart filled with a happiness that I couldn't express. I thanked God for helping us and for giving us the courage to start and to keep going.

Ben and I had launched our business without knowing much about either restaurants or financial balance sheets. We would keep on learning as we went along. I knew that the Dwarf Grill (later called the Dwarf House) would succeed. It made a profit from the first week we opened. Sales at the restaurant have risen *every year since then*, more than four decades of continual increase in customers and sales. Our tag was "Good Food Is Good Health." Another saying we used was "Food is the staff of life—therefore, make it good."

As we blessed others, we ourselves were blessed, in fulfillment of Proverbs 11:25, "He who waters will also be watered himself." It's an axiom of business that if you help people get what they want, you'll get what you want.

That tiny restaurant—built with used nails and wood, four refurbished tables and assorted chairs, and ten stools at a counter surrounding secondhand equipment—was my launching pad. I was taking my first steps as an adult in the business world.

Six days a week, twenty-four hours a day, we remained open to serve our growing family of patrons. One time I spent thirty-six hours behind the counter. I rented a room next door so that later when I got some help, I could run over there, sleep for a few hours, and be on call in case I was needed in a hurry.

A hamburger cost fifteen cents. Bacon and tomato sandwiches cost twenty-five cents; we served a deluxe steak sandwich for thirty cents. Our bacon and eggs cost thirty cents, and fried ham went for twenty-five cents. Homemade pies, ten cents a slice; Cokes, five cents, served from the bottle with a glass of ice.

One of Ben's hobbies was flying. He and our brother Horace earned their pilot's licenses and rented planes quite regularly to fly around the South.

On July 19, 1949, Ben worked at the Dwarf House until 3:00 P.M. He and Horace and two friends arranged to rent a Cessna 170. It was a typically beautiful July day in Georgia. The temperature reached the high eighties, and billowy clouds had moved in by early afternoon, hinting of rain within the next few hours.

My brothers and their friends took off for Chattanooga, even though bad weather had started moving our way sooner than expected. They landed at Rome, Georgia, because they didn't want to take a chance of getting caught in a severe storm in their light plane.

An hour after sundown, the storm had passed over Rome, and they received clearance to proceed to Chattanooga. They flew over Chatsworth, Georgia, heading toward Dalton. Someone spotted their plane shortly after 8:00 P.M. The plane caught his attention because of its low altitude and blinking lights on the wings. The man phoned the state patrol and reported seeing an SOS signal.

Neither Ben nor Horace was licensed for instrument flying. The plane was equipped only for visual flying, and we assume they decided to land. Their distress signal put the state patrol into action. Although they could not tell the size of the plane, one patrol car set up a spotlight in what they called an auxiliary field, near Dalton, Georgia. Another trooper called local residents and asked, "Will you come out here with your automobiles and shine your headlights on the field so that this fellow can see to land?"

All over the county, people headed toward the airstrip. A patrolman at the entrance directed traffic, filling up two sides of the field. They hoped they could get the cars there soon enough to provide adequate light for landing.

"There it is!"

"He's coming in!"

Everyone could hear the engine and watched intently as the plane descended slowly.

"He's going to make it!" some shouted.

The plane came within five feet of the ground, but then the wingtip grazed a patrol car's radio antenna. Ben or Horace or one of their friends—we don't know which one was flying the plane at that point—gunned the engine to go back up and try one more time. Just as he did so, the engine sputtered and died with the plane perhaps thirty feet above the ground.

"It fell like a pancake," one observer told us. "One minute it was edging upward, and the noise of the engine filled the air. The next moment the engine coughed and stopped, and then seconds later that plane just fell straight to the ground."

The Cessna burst into flames on impact. The intense heat prevented anyone from getting close. By the time the fire was put out, the charred remains inside the plane were barely recognizable.

Both of my brothers were dead—my only brothers, taken in a single accident. When I opened the daily report book on Monday morning, I read the figures in Ben's handwriting. His death hit me forcefully for the second time. Writing those numbers was the last thing he had done at the Dwarf House. Ben would never figure the daily receipts again. My brother was gone.

My tears gushed out. I couldn't stop them. Despite

our differences in temperament and interests, I had loved my younger brother.

A year after Ben's death, I bought out his share of the business from his wife, Eunice. For several years afterward, I saw to it that Eunice and her daughter, Nancy, were provided for.

Loyal customers made the Dwarf Grill grow into what was later to be called the Dwarf House. Word of mouth in the food business is more important than any other source of advertising. It's better to maintain your present customers than to spend a lot of time and expense replacing them with new ones.

I tell our Operators at Chick-fil-A Units today: Consistency is one of the most important aspects of the food business. You can even build your business on bad coffee as long as you're consistent. Customers are very sensitive to change.

One time we decided to serve a pat of butter with the toast instead of buttering the toast at the grill. Our customers didn't like that one bit.

"Hey," they would say, "we want you to butter that toast before you serve it, just like you always did before."

It doesn't take much to turn a customer off.

The friendliness of the staff . . . the expression on your face . . . paying attention to their special requests—all these are extremely important. People don't always go out to eat because they're hungry. They may be simply looking for fellowship or a pleasant experience. Beyond serving food, we try to meet their emotional needs and sometimes talk to them about their spiritual needs as well. Our Lord conducted much of His teaching around a dining table.

If a customer isn't satisfied, he doesn't complain; he just doesn't come back. He may be too embarrassed to complain, afraid the staff will think he's trying to get out of paying for his food.

One day a long-time customer at the Dwarf House couldn't start her car. She asked a young shift manager if she could use the phone to call a garage. He refused to give her permission so she phoned me and told me she would never come back to the Dwarf House again. That young manager had to learn that the customers are right *all* the time. They are our bosses, and sometimes they are quite entertaining, as the following stories show.

One morning a customer who had been eating with us a long time brought in his own sausage for breakfast. Someone had given him "country fresh sausage," and he wanted me to put it on the grill and serve it with his eggs.

I put our regular sausage on the grill and served it with his eggs. He couldn't brag enough about his wonderful find. I let him rave on for a while, and when he had finished, I gave him back his sausage and told him he had been eating ours as usual.

Two guys used to come in early for breakfast together. One would order two scrambled eggs and bacon. The second guy would say, "Give me the same thing, but instead of two eggs, just give me one. Instead of scrambling, make it over light. And instead of bacon, give me sausage."

When we built a new restaurant in 1967 on the same property behind the original restaurant, we designed a four-foot red door at the entrance "for dwarfs and little folks" to enter. Of course, all the children would drag their parents and grandparents through that four-foot door just for fun. Sometimes big, tough truck drivers get a thrill out of stooping to enter through that door.

We are currently expanding the Dwarf House concept, along with the Chick-fil-A Unit in malls across the United States and free-standing Chick-fil-A restaurants. Four links in the Dwarf House chain have already been established, and the prospects look good for more of them to take their places alongside Chick-fil-A Units. More than forty years have passed since we first flipped on the neon sign and opened our doors to serve "the staff of life" to our customers.

4

CRISIS IS OPPORTUNITY IN DISGUISE

A *Chinese parable tells a perceptive story* about a rural family long, long ago. The family had a horse that helped to plow the land and raise their food.

One day the horse ran away while the farmer's son was plowing in the field. Neighbors came and said to the old man and the boy, "We heard about your bad luck. It is so bad."

"How do you know it is bad?" answered the farmer. "It is not over yet."

Sure enough, in a few days the horse came back leading a herd of wild horses.

"We heard about your good luck and came to congratulate you," said the neighbors.

"How do you know it is good luck?" answered the farmer. "It is not over yet."

A few days later while the boy was trying to train one of the horses, it threw him and broke his leg.

"Oh," said the neighbors, "we heard about your bad luck and came to sympathize."

Again the old man replied, "How do you know it is bad? It is not over yet."

The parable ends by saying that a great war came, and all the able-bodied young men were taken off to fight. But the boy with the broken leg stayed at home and cared for his aging father for the rest of his days.

When I went to sleep that cold night of February 23, 1960, I had no reason to think that my life would change radically within the next few hours. I had opened the first Dwarf House in 1946 and the second one in 1951. Both restaurants were doing extremely well. If I had any complaint, it was simply that the two of them kept me too busy. For a long time, I had been under a strain, but then so were a lot of men my age in those years after World War II.

I was awakened at 1:30 A.M. on February 24, 1960, to be told, "Mr. Cathy, your restaurant in Forest Park is on fire."

"How bad?" I asked, thinking it might be a nightmare. A nightmare it was.

I jumped into my trousers. Jeannette was awake by this time and began to ask questions.

"Whoever called said that it looked pretty bad," I told my wife.

As I dressed, all sorts of things went through my mind: *Maybe it isn't so bad . . . wonder how it started . . . how much insurance do I have . . . suppose it's real bad, what will I do?* Having never experienced a fire, I thought of various dire possibilities. Outside it was a cold six degrees Fahrenheit, unusually cold for the Atlanta area. What a time to have a fire! Well, you don't pick a time for a fire—ever!

I live about twenty miles from the Forest Park loca-

*———————————————————

*Winners concentrate
on winning.
Losers concentrate
on getting by.*

———————————————————

tion. By the time I reached Morrow, five miles away, I saw for certain that the fire was severe. The sky was aglow as if great furnace doors had been opened. My heart started beating harder. I pressed down further on the acclerator and finally arrived at the scene.

Firemen were swarming all over the place. Their water hoses lay tangled like a bunch of snakes. Policemen were detouring what little traffic crept by at that time of the morning. The officers recognized me and let me through.

Flames were shooting high into the air. The Forest Park firemen, along with those from the nearby army depot, were fighting vigorously. Fire Chief Joe Piccard was on the scene giving directions to his men and trying to talk with me. He said it appeared that the fire started in the storage area in the center of the building. He advised me to stay at least one hundred feet away. How I wanted to head into that fire and pull a few things out to safety, but I could not.

Soon the roof began to groan, and in a moment it crashed to the floor of the inferno. Firemen had to use great caution to keep from getting burned.

One by one, employees began to show up as they were notified of the fire. They came to help, but who could help when it appeared that everything was destroyed?

By daybreak, the fire was under control. Customers stopping by for breakfast seemed almost as concerned as I was when they saw what had happened. Many people came by just to express their condolences. A few remarked, "Guess you have plenty of insurance. . . ."

I didn't.

My first move was to take possession of the night's receipts, which had been secured in a metal file box—all okay. When the sun came up, James Martin, Charlie Sealock, and other employees began to pull out usable food and transfer it to the Dwarf House in Hapeville.

Several builders in the area got together and said, "Truett, we will co-op our efforts and have you back in business in thirty days."

I should have taken them up on their offer, but I didn't. I had only $25,000 worth of insurance, an amount grossly inadequate to rebuild. I began to question why God had let this happen. Everything had fallen into place up until this time. I didn't know where to start to put things right.

On February 25, the day after the fire, I mentioned to Jeannette that I had passed some blood. She insisted I should go to a doctor, so I made an appointment with Dr. Allen Smith (not his real name). He sent me to a clinic for tests, which showed that I had polyps in the colon and would require surgery to remove them.

"Doc," I objected, "I can't do it now. I have to rebuild my restaurant."

Dr. Smith knew about the fire because he was a regular customer and his office was in Forest Park. "You had better forget the restaurant and think about yourself," he warned. "Surgery is not all that bad. You could be back on limited duty within thirty days."

The doctor and Jeannette insisted, so I agreed. My plan was to make a speedy recovery and "get on with it," but things didn't work out as I thought.

My surgery was scheduled for what turned out to be a really cold day following an ice storm in the night. Jeannette put chains on the car's tires and arrived at the hospital around daybreak, just before I was to go down for surgery. Hospital attendants had given me an anesthetic to prepare me for surgery, but because of the icy roads hospital personnel, including the surgeon, were not able to make it in on time for work. The operation was postponed until the middle of the afternoon. Jeannette stayed by my side to encourage me and pray with me. Our pastor came and tried to comfort me. He prayed, too, but I didn't feel calm when they finally wheeled me down the hallway.

The surgery went fine, but I awoke in my room with great pain.

"You're not allergic to codeine, are you?" a nurse asked as she prepared my arm for an injection.

"I don't suppose I am," I replied. "I've never had codeine before."

Jeannette held my hand as I lay waiting for the codeine to take effect. The pain became a dull ache, but instead of getting sleepy, I began to feel fidgety. No position was comfortable. By the time Jeannette called the nurse back, I was thrashing around and gritting my teeth. I bit the inside of my mouth and had to restrain myself from yelling. This led to uncontrollable hiccups until a stomach pump inserted through my nostrils removed the offending codeine to which I was indeed allergic. They put that burning tube in my stomach a second time. By morning my temperature had shot up, but I felt as though I was freezing. I wanted to die, but then with my next breath, I was afraid I *would* die.

"Call Dr. Smith," Jeannette firmly demanded.

The nurse returned. "Dr. Smith has gone for the weekend," she reported. "We're trying to locate him now for further instructions."

For two weeks I remained in an unstable condition, but my doctor decided I would feel better at home, so he released me. I had no energy even to think about my one restaurant, let alone direct a rebuilding project for the second.

In my absence, the employees took hold beautifully. They pulled a cookwagon onto the site, erected a tent, and were once again serving food under our sign, "The world's best hamburgers in Forest Park."

Cultivating good relationships with people in the community had paid off. The local newspapers gave us a lot of publicity. We hired car hostesses to take drive-in orders and serve people as they sat in their automobiles.

The more I thought of rebuilding the same facility, the more restless I became to operate a self-serve restaurant. We built a temporary Dwarf House on the foundation of the original building, and this time we divided the space so that my sister, Gladys Garr, could operate a gift shop in the front.

Six months passed, and it was time for me to go back for a medical checkup.

"How are you feeling?" the doctor asked as he began his examination.

"Fine," I replied. "I'm fully recovered." But my elation didn't last long.

"The polyps have grown back," the doctor told me.

I could hardly believe what he was saying. I groaned, "I can't go through that again."

"The first surgeon decided to clip the polyps," he said patiently. "That's easier on the patient, and usually it's enough to take care of the polyps. This time I suggest removing about twelve inches of the colon."

Before I could respond, he added, "Mr. Cathy, most of us have about four and a half feet of the large intestine. We can cut out about twelve inches, and you'll never know the difference."

"But what if they grow back again?"

"Not likely to happen, especially this way. The polyps grew back in the same area. We want to remove that entire section."

Dr. Martin scheduled me for surgery in two days to reduce the agony of suspense. That evening as I drove home I hardly noticed anything. I sat for a long time in the driveway staring at our lovely house and the beautiful, quiet grounds. I thought of our horses and of all the plans I'd made for the children to enjoy the open spaces. But I knew I wouldn't be alive to share it with them. In my mind I walked all through the 262 acres. At thirty-eight years of age, I owned more in that one piece of property than my parents ever had in their entire lives.

Slowly I got out of the car, feeling as if I were a hundred years old. I went inside the house and tried to hide my anxieties from the children. I wanted to enjoy being with them. As we played together the rest of the day, more than once I thought, *I'll never pick up Dan and Bubba again. I'll never have Trudy's tiny fingers take mine and pull on my arm as we walk together.*

That night Jeannette and I talked together for a long time. She knew I expected to die in the hospital, but she didn't give in to my discouragement.

"Truett," she said, "God isn't finished with your life yet. I don't think He's going to take you."

I would have given anything to believe those words. As we drove to Emory Hospital the following morning, I would have given every dime I had not to go back into surgery. I realized the insignificance of material things.

As we drove, a strange thing happened. It began with a simple thought: *It doesn't matter whether I live or die. I have peace with God.* Worry and fear vanished. I still believed I would die, but it no longer mattered because I had prepared myself and I was ready.

Jeannette's face was the first thing I saw when I opened my eyes. She bent down and kissed me. "You're going to be all right," she whispered as I went back into a deep sleep. Each time I awakened that day, I could hardly believe that I was still alive. Each day that I could, I visited the hospital chapel and stared at a cross mounted on an altar. I couldn't find words to express my gratitude. In my heart I kept saying, *I'm alive! Thank You, God, that I'm alive.*

No matter what lay in the future, I knew I could face it.

I went ahead with my plans to be the first to introduce self-serve fast food to Forest Park, convinced that it was the wave of the future. I had gone to Chicago to study the Li'l Abner Restaurant chain and watch its operation. I didn't like cooking food ahead of time and having it ready for pickup, but I knew our nation was increasingly time conscious and would soon demand such service.

Our new building at Forest Park looked beautiful. It had a kind of umbrella shape, a modern design with bright colors. I went $90,000 into debt, the most money I had ever borrowed.

A local pastor told me at our dedication ceremony, "Truett, this business will never fail because you have dedicated it to the Lord."

Jack Troy, a local newspaper publisher, devoted an entire sixteen-page tabloid section to his newspaper featuring my new fast-food, self-serve restaurant. For three days we celebrated, giving away prizes and enjoying special music. A local station presented marathon radio coverage. But something was wrong.

As soon as our customers came inside, I directed them to the self-service counter, a new experience for them and for us.

"We'll keep coming," some said, "but we don't like it." Others told me, "We'll eat at the Hapeville Dwarf House." Still others said nothing, but I knew what they were thinking.

I invited my friend Ted Davis over for a look. He had been in the restaurant business far longer than I, so we sat and watched the operation for an hour.

"Truett," he said, "you'll lose some customers because you've changed things, but you'll gain others."

But I didn't want to lose *any* customers. In time, I leased the building to Ted because he wanted to bring Kentucky Fried Chicken to Atlanta. Ted invited me to go into partnership with him, but I didn't because the restaurant would have to stay open on Sunday.

"Truett, Sunday is *the* day for chicken," he said. "Women are tired of cooking all week. They can send their husbands out for fried chicken, or they can pick it up on their way to picnics."

I wasn't thinking about chicken then. I had other, more important problems.

"If you change your mind," he said, "I'm convinced there's a real future in linking up with Kentucky Fried Chicken."

"Maybe you're right," I said.

And, of course, he was right. The franchise did well for Ted at my location. It also paid off the mortgage note and got me out from under all that pressure.

I was back where I had started with one restaurant. I said to Jeannette, "This time I'm going to stick right here. We're doing good business, and it'll give me a lot more free time."

But I grew restless. One day I took a long, hard look at the chicken on our Dwarf House menu, and things began to happen. I had introduced a chicken sandwich on the menu, and that single item was now opening up a new world of opportunity for me and my family and eventually for thousands of our associates in the enterprise called Chick-fil-A.

How I got the name, how the logo was developed, and how the restaurants were built are subjects of another chapter. What we looked upon as a crisis in Forest Park, which we would have done much to avoid, became a golden opportunity in disguise.

Was it going to be easier to succeed than to fail? Time would tell.

5

OBSERVING THE FOURTH COMMANDMENT

When *Saturday came during our first* week of business back there in 1946, Ben and I sank exhausted into a couple of chairs after the dinner crowd had thinned. Between the two of us, we had covered six twenty-four-hour shifts.

"What do you think, Truett?" my brother asked.

"I think we ought to close tomorrow," I replied.

The thought of working around the clock on Sunday and then starting all over again on Monday was just too much. From then on, we told customers, "We're open twenty-four hours a day, but not on Sunday."

Closing on Sunday has become a distinctive principle of my Christian background. From my infancy, my Sunday school teachers and pastors stressed that Sunday is the Lord's Day. I see another reason. God commanded, "Six days you shall labor and do all your work" (Exod. 20:9). God told the Israelites to work only six days so that the seventh could be used for rest.

God blessed the seventh day and sanctified it, set it aside. The book of Genesis describes the seventh day as a very, very special day. It is made for man, not man for it.

While I was growing up, Sunday was an important day for family times together; often Mom and Dad would take us to visit kinfolks. I believe God gave His laws not to make life hard but to make it better. Our bodies and our minds need time off to recharge. I've accepted that as a principle and honored God by doing it. God has honored us and the business because of it.

How could I teach the thirteen-year-old boys in my Sunday school class to observe the Lord's Day if my cash registers were jingling at my restaurants?

Although we've been closing my places of business for more than forty years, I keep hearing the same comments and questions:

"Look at all the business you're losing." That's the most common one. I don't believe we've lost any sales in the long run. In the shopping malls where we locate our Chick-fil-A restaurants, we usually generate more sales per square foot in six days than many others do in seven.

We also believe that by giving employees that free day, we attract the kind of people who want Sunday off because of their own convictions. People who take a day of rest to worship the Lord and to refresh themselves spiritually and physically are the kind of associates we seek.

I don't oppose others who stay open. In fact, Jeannette and I nearly always eat Sunday dinner in someone else's restaurant. I tease her from time to time because she once promised, "I'll cook you three meals a day every day if you'll just take me out to eat on Sunday."

I have been criticized for patronizing restaurants on Sunday. Folks have said it's hypocritical and incon-

*—————————

*Profits should
be the* score
*of the game,
not the* name
of the game.

—————————

sistent with my convictions. Maybe someday I'll grow in my spiritual development to wholly reverence the Lord's Day. Possibly my witness is weakened among some people because of my eating out on Sunday.

In early 1982, I received a letter from a developer whose mall is among the largest shopping centers in the U.S. "We are most pleased to have a Chick-fil-A Unit," he began. Then came the pressure. Part of his letter is quoted below:

We have run surveys of people in the —— Center Mall on Sunday afternoon and we have found that almost 100% of those who come from church to the center said they came because coming to the mall was recreation for them. . . . They eat lunch in the mall. They sit on the benches and in our pleasant garden areas. They very much enjoy their visits to the mall. They park free. They pay nothing to come to the mall. . . . We deeply respect your principles which motivate you to want Chick-fil-A to be closed on Sunday. In all our other 350 or so leases, the tenants must be open on Sunday. We accepted your lease because you felt strongly on that issue and we respected you for it.

I understand that your main reasons for closing on Sunday are to permit your people to honor the Sabbath and have a day of rest. The purpose of this long letter to you is to call to your attention the following:

1. Our surveys indicate churchgoers are very happy to have us open on Sunday afternoon so they can come here after church at no cost.

2. We reason that it is appropriate for us to

ask some of our people to work on Sunday because, by virtue of the need to have a place for
thousands of people to come to on Sunday, our
mall has become an essential service just as is a
drug store or filling station.

3. Your Chick-fil-A facility employs clean-cut
young people. We have interviewed some of the
young people who go to school five days per week
and work in other ——— Center food operations
on Saturday and Sunday. Many of these young people work on the weekends to save toward their college education. It is very possible that many of
these young people will be able to go to college
only if they are permitted to work on Saturdays
and Sundays, which are the only days they do not
attend school. (Their Sunday workday does not
start until after church.)

We would appreciate your giving our letter
some deep thought. I ask that you consider opening Sunday afternoons so the Chick-fil-A could
fulfill the same function as does ——— Center's—
that is, provide an essential service for people who
want to eat out on Sunday. (Our surveys indicate
that a major reason for families eating out on Sunday is so the mother and wife can rest.) We would
further suggest that only those who volunteer
work on Sunday afternoon.

We would be happy for you to try Sunday
afternoon openings and for you to feel free to revert
back at any time to closing, if you wish.

Your facility is most attractive. You have very
tasty products. We have thousands of store employees and Sunday afternoon strollers who are being

denied the right to eat in your place on Sunday afternoons. We hope you will give deep consideration to this. . . .

If you feel that the points we set forth in this letter are valid (and you will consider keeping Chick-fil-A open on Sunday in ——— Center) we would like to offer our contribution in the amount of $5,000 to the churches or organizations of your choice.

My reply to this gentleman went as follows:

Thank you for your kind and well-worded letter. I'm sure you were speaking your conviction in a generous way and I respect you and what you had to say.

Let me first thank you for permitting us to close on Sunday. We're doing business on your premises and you did not have to make an exception. Because of this, we'll pledge to you exceptional performance during the six days we are open.

Why do we close on Sunday? Well, it all started back in 1946, when I opened my first restaurant, a 24-hour coffee shop called "The Dwarf House." After the first week, I determined that if it took seven days a week to make a living, I should be in some other business. Too, it was my conscience that I had to live with; I just never could come to the idea of dealing with money on the Lord's Day. I became a Christian at age 12; that's not to say that everything I've done since that time is becoming to a Christian, but I believe the Lord has blessed us because we recognize Him on this special day we call Sunday. Since establishing that policy in the beginning of my business life, we have not varied— and dare not.

If there is any business that is justified in opening on Sunday, I think it is the food business. We eat out often on Sunday after church and find it a great convenience (especially my wife). I do not condemn a businessperson for opening on Sunday; it is just a principle I stand very firmly on for my business.

We have 237 shopping center locations [approximately 400 as of this date and many more are planned], all closed on Sunday. Since I don't like to eat at the same place all the time, I say let the people eat some place else on Sunday. You may check us out, but in the vast majority of the malls we are in, we are "No. 1" in sales in food, and in many malls, "No. 1" in sales overall tenant mix, even though we do not open on Sunday.

We find closing on Sunday attracts those people who give attention to spiritual growth and are family oriented. The fact that we have Sunday closing helps attract quality housewives and young people as employees. (We offer a $1,000 scholarship to our young people working two or more years. To date, more than $1 million has been awarded.) [This figure is now over the $5 million mark.]

. . . Your thoughts are well received. You are just the kind of person we would like to honor with any reasonable request, but please understand, we cannot compromise on certain principles.

Thank you for including us in your mall and for permitting us to remain closed on Sundays. When you are in Atlanta, please come by and give me the opportunity to meet you personally.

We have it written in our lease with each shopping center that *all* Chick-fil-A restaurants be permitted to remain closed on Sunday. Some developers inject in their lease that Chick-fil-A may close on Sunday "as long as *all* Units are closed on Sunday." *One* Operator could cause us a lot of problems over that issue. And in one instance, an Operator did cause us trouble.

It started when we received disturbing reports from several people. "I thought you never opened on Sunday," a friend said.

"We don't," I replied, "and never will."

"I saw one of your stores open on a Sunday afternoon," our friend said, and he named the place.

He's mistaken, I thought, but I passed the word on to Jimmy Collins, then Chick-fil-A's executive vice president.

"I've heard the same report from two other people," Jimmy said. "I'll find out the truth."

Jimmy dialed the store. A young man answered. "What are your store hours on Sunday?" he asked, not identifying himself.

"Twelve to six."

"Thank you," Jimmy said and hung up.

The next morning Jimmy told me about his phone call. I thought about it a few seconds. I wanted to be sure of what had happened. The month had almost come to an end.

"Let's wait until we get this month's report," I

said. I decided that if the Operator wrote down sales for Sunday, I could believe he had not understood our iron-clad policy of never opening on Sunday. I wanted to give him every possible benefit of the doubt. "But if he doesn't show sales for Sunday, then we'll know."

A few days later, Jimmy brought in the monthly report. The Operator had not listed the Sunday business. He had, apparently, divided his sales between Saturday and Monday. We believed the totals came out right, but he had broken a trust with us and had violated one of the company's basic policies.

We called him to Atlanta and terminated his Operator's Agreement. "I'm not dismissing you for opening the store on Sunday," I told him. "I'm terminating you for deceiving us. Your records are not true. You have lied to us, and that's why we're asking you to leave."

One other fact made this painful to deal with. When that Operator came to work for Chick-fil-A, he told me, "I'm the director of music in our church. I'm pleased that you never open on Sunday because I'll still be the music director for our church."

In March 1984, I received a letter from a Christian man. I'm quoting it in its entirety because of its interesting content:

Dear Mr. Cathy:

This is a letter of repentance and apology, though we have never met or had communications or dealings of any sort.

It is occasioned because of my rashness in concluding, and in stating several times to individuals and groups of Christians, that there is an inconsistency of witness and deed in your business relationship with Chick-fil-A and your involvement with the Lord's Day Alliance.

I again made that observation last Sunday morning before a Bible class and several members advised me quickly that I am in error, that your restaurants are not open on Sundays as I had believed. (Obviously, I am not one of your regular customers.)

I never enjoy being wrong, but in this case I am in a very real sense delighted to know that you have not, as so many of us professed Christians, compromised your convictions on this matter for economic gain.

I thus ask your forgiveness, as I have asked the Lord's, and encourage you in your walk of the Christian way.

May you and yours always enjoy the greatest blessings of God's service. Let Christ be Lord!

Never have I intended to make a big issue out of being closed on Sunday. It amazes me that other people bring up the subject so often. In almost any gathering when anyone mentions Chick-fil-A, someone says, "And you know, they always close on Sunday."

On the first day of the week, the early disciples gathered to commemorate the rising of Christ from the dead. What better reason can we have for doing the same? This is the formula God has given us for success. In this case it is *definitely* easier to succeed than to work seven days a week and miss the blessing.

To get his goodnight kiss he stood
    Beside my chair one night
And raised an eager face to me,
    A face with love alight.

And as I gathered in my arms
    The son God gave to me,
I thanked the lad for being good,
    And hoped he'd always be.

His little arms crept round my neck,
    And then I heard him say
Four simple words I can't forget—
    Four words that made me pray.

They turned a mirror on my soul,
    On secrets no one knew,
They startled me, I hear them yet:
    He said, "I'll be like you."*

*Herbert Parker, *These Times*, June 1979.

6

LET GOD PICK YOUR MATE

Next to a person's salvation and the choice of Christ as Master, the most important decision is choosing your mate. It's not as important to *find* the right mate as it is to prepare yourself to *be* the right mate, though. If you prepare yourself, eventually you and your future mate will find each other.

Marriage is a lifetime commitment to be taken seriously. I heard a Christian psychologist say that too often people marry hoping it will bring them happiness. But it's not designed that way. Marriage is to make a person complete. Marriage is not taking; it's 100 percent giving. The honeymoon is wonderful, but when it's over, you have to go back to work, pay the bills, and see the other person in less-than-complimentary ways.

The daughter of one of our restaurant Operators asked her parents if her boyfriend could work at the Unit during the summer vacation period. They were not excited about the boy, but they hired him to honor the request of their daughter. After the girl worked around that young fellow for a while, she saw things in him that she didn't like either. His performance, language, and attitude showed her another side of him. Seeing a person perform in the real world, especially under pressure, is quite different from seeing that person sitting in a convertible under a full moon.

Marriage can make you or break you. Bathe the matter in prayer. Look at it from all aspects.

In 1948, I was married at 26 to a girl it seems I have always known. My first vivid remembrance of her is from 1929 when I was eight years old. She was a year younger than I, a dainty girl with bright, expressive eyes and a sweetness that made me feel good when I was near her.

From infancy, Jeannette McNeil went to church with family members at West End Baptist Church, which I, too, attended. When she was old enough, we walked to church together. At age nine, Jeannette understood her need for a personal relationship with God. She responded to an invitation one day and received Christ as her Savior. She may have understood little more than that "Jesus loves me, this I know," and that when she did wrong, God forgave her. But from then on, Jeannette's life revolved around Jesus Christ and the church.

I never had a point where I could say, "Suddenly I understood the Bible," or "At that moment I knew God's love." I have no idea what it would be like *not* to attend church every Sunday because I have done it all my life and I enjoy the study of God's Word and the association with other believers.

Jeannette sometimes came to our house in those days, but she doesn't have much memory of me. I was shy and awkward and seldom said anything more to her than "Hello." But even then, the first stirrings of love were growing in me, and I had already planned

*———————————————

*Associate yourselves
only with
those people you can
be proud of
whether they work
for you or you work
for them.*

———————————————

that when I grew up, I would marry Jeannette or someone just like her.

We both attended Joe Brown Junior High School in Atlanta. Then, in the ninth grade, Jeannette moved out of the neighborhood. She attended the Girls' High School, and I went to Commercial High, later to Tech High School. We didn't see much of each other during the next few years. I didn't have time or money for dating. I took out a few girls, but I never got serious with any of them.

I have to thank my sister Gladys for bringing us together in later years. Gladys, the youngest of my sisters but five years older than I, kept in contact with Jeannette through the years.

"I was in Woolworth's today and guess who I bumped into?" she'd say as we sat at the table.

"Who?" I'd ask.

"Jeannette McNeil." Then she'd give us all the available news.

In the spring of 1947, Gladys (by then Mrs. Lamar Garr) told me, "Truett, Jeannette McNeil's home for Easter, and I'm going to have her over for supper."

She talked a little about her and then said, "I thought I'd ask our whole family, too."

I must have given myself away by my eager response because as we talked, Gladys finally said, "Say, Truett, she's coming here on the trolley, but why don't you take her home in your car?"

"She wouldn't want me to drive her home," I objected.

"Sure she would. Just ask her."

"Why don't you ask her for me?"

"Okay," Gladys promised. "When I see it's getting

time for her to go home, I'll say something like, 'Truett, why don't you give Jeannette a ride home in your car?' How does that sound?"

"Sounds fine to me," I said.

By then, Jeannette had completed college and was attending the New Orleans Baptist Seminary. I wanted to see her, but I tortured myself with questions and doubts. Ben and I had been in business a full year and were making a profit, although I still worked eighteen hours a day. I kept thinking, *Jeannette won't be interested in me. She's probably already fallen in love with some seminary student.*

Jeannette had gone to work immediately after high school, but she always wanted to go on to college. With help from friends in the West End Church and work scholarships, she went to Tift College in Forsyth, Georgia and later to the New Orleans Baptist Seminary.

I took her home that night on schedule in my new, off-white 1947 Chevrolet that I had purchased less than a month before her visit. She commented on the nice car, and I blushed with pride.

She didn't mention having any special boyfriends. I still felt awkward, but I knew then that I was in love with Jeannette. I was twenty-six years old, and I wanted to marry her. I didn't tell her that, but I knew that in love, as in business, you have to go after what you want.

Months later I decided to visit her at school in New Orleans. I took her mother along in the car so that she could also enjoy a visit with her daughter. It also strengthened my chance to get to visit her.

Jeannette and I talked about many things while I was there on campus with her—the seminary, the classes, and other students. I wanted to be sure she had no other student in mind as a prospective husband. I asked her a lot of questions, trying to keep them general. Jeannette was determined to marry only the man who was God's choice for her.

I spent as much time as possible with Jeannette during those two days. Her mother was there, too, but I didn't mind because I was near Jeannette. I sensed that, for the first time, she had started to think of me as someone other than just a friend.

We left for Atlanta after breakfast on the third day. Jeannette's mother was sitting in the car when I said, "I just want to talk to you alone for a minute, Jeannette."

She smiled, and we held hands as we walked along the driveway. I told her how much I had enjoyed being with her. Then I handed her an envelope.

"What's this?"

"Never mind right now," I said. "Don't open it until after I'm gone."

"Aren't you going to at least tell me what's in it?"

"No. You'll find out after we're on our way back to Atlanta."

Before leaving home, I had bought her a round-trip ticket by air to Atlanta so she could come home for Easter vacation. Almost by the time Mrs. McNeil and I returned to Atlanta, I had a letter from her. The ticket had overwhelmed her. She had initial reservations about accepting the gift, yet she did want to come home. And she added, "I want to see you again."

She looked wonderful to me when I saw her walk across the concourse. The plane had pitched and plunged through rough weather and had made its passengers airsick. Jeannette walked off that plane, thankful to be on the ground, and she wondered if she would have the courage to fly again. But she recovered quickly, and we began to enjoy the Easter weekend together.

All that spring and into the summer months I worked long hours and tried to spend time with Jeannette as well. That left only one place to cut down: I slept less.

We did most of our courting in the restaurant. Since my restaurant was closed on the Lord's Day, we spent many Sunday evenings there, just the two of us. We'd play the jukebox, and I'd bring out the Cokes. We'd sit and talk, endlessly it seemed.

Some Sunday evenings we went to the Grace Methodist Church in Atlanta. Dr. Charles Allen, the pastor, did a series of sermons on courtship and marriage. The messages were so popular that people came from many churches, and we had to arrive at least twenty minutes early to get seats.

One Saturday I took the afternoon off. I picked up Jeannette, along with my sister Esther, and we drove to Chattanooga, Tennessee, about a two-hour trip north of Atlanta. We planned to see my married sister Myrtle who lived there, but I had something else in mind as well.

Esther stayed with Myrtle that afternoon while I took Jeannette to what I consider to be one of the most beautiful places in the world, Lookout Mountain, just outside Chattanooga. We strolled around and enjoyed the view and the quietness. We walked down a path and were pleased to see that few people were there that day. I found a secluded spot where we could chat a few minutes. Then I looked right into her eyes and said, "Jeannette, I love you. I think you know that pretty well by now. I want to marry you. Will you marry me?"

She didn't answer, and that surprised me. I was usually the one without words.

"I need to think about it," she finally said.

"You love me, don't you?"

"Oh, yes, Truett! I just need time to think about it. Marriage is forever."

"I want you to be sure, Jeannette." I had hoped she would say yes right away, but I was willing to wait.

"I don't want to make a mistake. I only plan to marry once, so I want to be sure it's right . . . for both of us."

Naturally I felt disappointed, but I also understood. She had not said no. And she loved me. For then, it was enough.

Sunday evening as we sipped Cokes together in the restaurant, Jeannette said, "Truett, I love you. I've thought and thought about us and prayed so much about us, especially since yesterday. Yes, I want to marry you."

We set September 19, 1948, as the date for our wedding. Even before proposing, I had a pretty good feeling that Jeannette loved me enough to marry me. Without telling her, I bought a piece of property on Sylvan Road in East Point so that I could build a house on it. The lot, 60 by 125 feet, was only three miles from the restaurant.

My brother Horace, before he lost his life in an airplane crash, worked as a machinist in the composing room of the *Atlanta Journal,* and in his off-hours he did construction work. I made an arrangement with

Horace, and he helped me build the house. I subcon-
tracted most of the worked, and we finished the house
on time. When we returned to Atlanta after our honeymoon, I took my bride to our house on Sylvan Road.

I can't remember being happier at any time in my
life. Everything was going right. In just over two years
the restaurant had become financially sound and was
doing extremely well. I was already trying to figure out
how to start a second one. Jeannette and I were as
happy as we could be. It was as though nothing could
go wrong. We had kept ourselves for each other, and we
would remember for a lifetime our wedding vows. But
if we thought we were happy alone, we would also experience the supreme joys that children bring to a Christian home.

When it comes to living clean and saving oneself
for marriage to that special person, the theme of my
book is many times stronger: It is easier to succeed
than to fail.

7

MAKE FIRESIDE
AN EARLY HEAVEN

The children of Christian homes around the world shine as beacons in a dark world. Jeannette and I are privileged to have three children and ten grandchildren. We have raised our youngsters on a 262-acre farm in Clayton County, twenty miles from my corporate office in south Atlanta.

It was fun to see Dan (1953), Donald—"Bubba"—(1954), and Trudy (1955) as little children running about, poking with curiosity into strange places . . . shrieking with delight over the merest trifle . . . and learning about God through the world He has created, in the eternal record He has given, and at the hearthside, which is an early foretaste of heaven itself.

I can still hear our children singing excitedly down on the farm:

> God's beautiful world,
> God's beautiful world,
>   I love God's beautiful world.
> He made it for you.
> He made it for me.
>   I love God's beautiful world.*

*From *Songs We Sing*, compiled by Mattie C. Leatherwood. © Copyright 1939. Renewal 1967 The Sunday School Board of the Southern Baptist Convention. All rights reserved. Used by permission.

While Dan, Bubba, and Trudy were still small enough for Jeannette to dress them up as dwarfs, we would stand them on the counter, and they would sing the "Dwarf House Jingle" with words by Ruby Graham sung to the tune of "Hey, Look Me Over!":

Hi! Take the family out for a treat
Bring them to the Dwarf House for the best to
    eat.
The most modern building, finest homemade
    pies,
Delicious steak plates served with salad and
    french fries,
The burgers best served anywhere, folks,

Made from the choicest U.S. grade meat,
And service to his family
And just cannot be beat.
Smiling dwarfs in to greet you wherever you
    may look,
So, folks, don't stay home and cook.

We have a dwarf mural moving on the wall,
Thick shakes and flavors and all the best of
    all,
So, whether you name is Smith, or even if it's
    Jones
We know you will love our chicken, folks,
    because it has no bones.

And we'll be mighty pleased for "checks";
    we'll think it is fine,
To have you come and see our patio and dine.

So, come out and treat the family to a feast fit
    for a king,
Where you choose the best of everything.

Come to the Dwarf House . . . and eat!

The possibilities for our children on the farm
seemed to be endless. They had ponies and horses to
ride as well as minibikes, go-carts, trail bikes, motorcycles, and tractors. They tended sheep and cattle, deer
and hogs. Often they would invite their friends to par-
ties in the barn or camp out in a field or climb into a
tree house to hide.

As marvelous as material blessings can be, it's still
true that the greatest gift to children is loving parents
living under one roof. People at all financial levels can
provide that. You cannot buy love and respect from
your children. You have to earn them by your conduct
and example. Parents are misled if they think that material gifts ensure a good relationship with their children.

Father is chairman of the board, president, and
chief executive officer in the world's greatest institution—the home. Mother is executive vice president in
charge of public relations, bookkeeping, interior deco-
rating, the commissary, infirmary, hospital, and all of
those things that make a house a home.

It is better to set an example rather than to enforce
a lot of rules. Parents have the responsibility of providing the physical, emotional, and spiritual needs of each
family member.

Concerned about his son, a father in our community asked his pastor to talk to the boy about the many temptations he will have to face as he grows older.

"Have *you* talked to your son?" the pastor asked.

"I'm ashamed to say this," the father replied, "but my life hasn't been a reflection of what I want my son to be. I'm fearful that any counsel I give my son would not be effective because of my personal conduct."

One day while I was flying from Pittsburgh, Pennsylvania, to Atlanta, I was seated beside a businessman from my city. He expressed great concern about his fifteen-year-old son and his seventeen-year-old daughter growing up in today's society.

He had ordered a beer from the stewardess, so after talking at length with him, I asked, "Do you encourage your children to drink beer?"

Children will do as their parents say until about the age of fourteen; from then on, they usually do as their parents do. My friend got the message instantly. He assured me that I had given him some food for thought. He thanked me sincerely as he left the plane and even wrote to thank me for bringing this to his attention.

Most Christian people like to say that they put God first, their family second, and themselves last. This sounds nice, but it isn't always practical. Occasionally in the crises of management, I must put business matters ahead of family association, but it should be the exception and not the rule. After all, a person's family knows as well as anyone that it is no great service to God or to them if the bread winner fails in business.

In addition to teaching my Sunday school class of boys, I also serve on the finance committee of our

*———————————

*The greatest gift
a mother and a dad
can give
to their children
is to love each other
and live together
under one roof.*

———————————

church. But sometimes it's necessary to put my business ahead of that. The way I look at it, you can't very well separate the three. It's a matter of judgment.

Of all the young people who are special to me, three are at the top of the list—Dan Truett, Donald Martin, and Trudy Ann Cathy. They were born close together, and that made life difficult for my wife. I probably failed Jeannette when the children were young by working too many hours at the restaurant and not lifting more of the load from her. That's one of my regrets. But I have always tried to let my children know how much I love them and how special they are.

I don't know if I was a strict father or not. My children knew what I expected of them, and I don't recall ever having to spend a lot of time trying to force them to understand.

Through the years, I observed certain mistakes other fathers made in giving their children, especially their sons, too much too soon. The automobile is usually the chief offender because it gives the young person a means of escape from family responsibility and influence.

I deliberately programmed my sons early about automobiles. When Dan was approximately ten years old and Bubba nine, I told them that if they waited until they reached eighteen to get a car, I would buy them a brand-new one of their choice. "Something within reason," I added.

From time to time I reminded them of my promise. They were free to borrow my car when they received their driver's licenses. "But you'll have to ask permission and tell me where you're going and what time

Along with his brother Ben *(left),* seventeen-year-old Truett *(second from right)* is an *Atlanta Journal* contest winner. Truett developed his flair for business early, first selling soft drinks at age eight and later magazines before beginning his daily paper route at age twelve.

After Truett graduated from high school, he was drafted into the U.S. Army. He served in ordnance until he was discharged in 1945.

This is where it all got started. Ben and Truett pooled resources and borrowed money to open the original Dwarf Grill on the south side of Atlanta in 1946. Hamburgers were fifteen cents, and Cokes, served from the bottle with a glass of ice, were a nickel. *Inset:* The newest Dwarf House in Jonesboro, Georgia, features waitress service, counter and table options, take-out service, and a drive-through window.

Jeannette coaches Don [Bubba], Dan, and Trudy as they sing the Dwarf House jingle for a radio commercial.

Brooksie Kirk *(l)*, Chick-fil-A's first employee, and Jeannette dress the part to help Truett cook and serve free samples of his new chicken sandwich at the Southeastern Restaurant Trade Show.

While Truett serves his famous Dwarfburger at the opening of the second Dwarf House, his sons Dan *(l)* and Don, dressed as dwarfs, entertain the customers.

Not only was the restaurant at Atlanta's Greenbriar Mall the first Chick-fil-A Unit, it pioneered the in-mall fast-food restaurant concept in 1967—an idea that caught on quickly in the years that followed.

Two years later, in 1969, the second Chick-fil-A restaurant opened in Savannah's Oglethorpe Mall.

Truett and Doris Williams, Chick-fil-A's first Operator, receive the "Choice in Chains Award" from Barry H. Reese, publisher of *Restaurants & Institutions* magazine.

Jeanette McGill and Truett listen as Don Perry, manager of public relations, takes to the microphone in celebration of the Chick-fil-A chain's twentieth anniversary.

Forty-six Chick-fil-A Operators and their spouses pose with their "Symbol of Success," awarded to Operators for achieving a 40 percent sales increase or $200,000 volume over the previous year.

Truett presents the keys to a brand-new Lincoln Mark VII to Joe Dinardo (l) and his wife Danie Lynn. Joe operates the Coastland Center restaurant in Naples, Florida.

Above: Truett surveys some of the dirt bikes and motorcycles he keeps on hand (l) for his young guests. When he's not selling chicken, he enjoys riding around his farm (r).

Truett's young friend Gene Hubbard enjoyed his last Christmas. Blind, deaf, and mute, Gene got around in a wheelchair after cancer was diagnosed and his left leg was amputated. Truett served as a pallbearer at Gene's funeral eight months after this photo was taken.

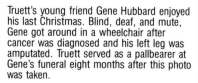

Students mill around Trustees Hall *(l)* at Berry College—ranked fifth nationally among colleges its size. Hermann Hall *(r)* houses the administrative offices, where Chick-fil-A, Inc., and Berry College entered into a unique partnership.

Full-time foster parents and up to twelve children live in Huddleston House on the WinShape Centre campus, located among the twenty-eight thousand acres of the Berry College complex.

A happy recipient of a $1,000 scholarship to the college of her choice. Each Chick-fil-A crew member who works at least twenty hours a week for two years and is recommended by his or her Operator is eligible. Scholarships totaling more than $5 million have been awarded since the program's inception in 1973.

Suthern O. Sims *(l),* president of Tift College in Forsyth, Georgia, posed with Truett after presenting him with an honorary Doctor of Commerce degree.

Jim Cumming *(l)*, owner of the building, and Truett display Atlanta's historical Flat Iron Building, the city's first skyscraper and location of Chick-fil-A's first downtown, non-mall restaurant.

When Truett attends the grand opening of a new Chick-fil-A restaurant, he doesn't stand around and watch!

Former President Jimmy Carter talks with Truett as he visits the new Chick-fil-A corporate headquarters.

Below: Plans call for a major expansion of Chick-fil-A's free-standing restaurant concept.

Situated on seventy-five wooded acres in southwest Atlanta, the new five-story headquarters building features an eighty-foot atrium lobby, skylighted roof, glass elevators, and a poured-in-place spiral staircase cantilevered over a fountain.

Ron Allen *(r)*, Delta Air Lines chairman and a regular breakfast customer, gives Truett a copy of the full-page color ad Delta placed in a local newspaper to celebrate the fortieth anniversary of the Dwarf House (his "favorite restaurant.")

Right: James L. S. Collins, who served as design consultant for Truett before becoming Chick-fil-A's third employee when he joined the infant company in 1968, is now president and chief operating officer.

Below: Truett receives the Silver Plate Award in the chain fast service category from International Foodservice Manufacturers Association; Hal Daugherty, *(l)*, chairman, and Michael Licata *(r)*, president.

"Choice in Chains": A National Family Opinion (NFO) mail survey from the largest consumer panel in America—representing 375,000 households—voted Chick-fil-A the #1 chicken chain in a survey sponsored by *Restaurants & Institutions* magazine.

Below: Truett is surrounded by some of his friends at a Chick-fil-A restaurant.

Chick-fil-A sponsors the concert tour of top female gospel artist Sandi Patti (*l*). The company also was the first corporate sponsor of the Gospel Music Association's Gospel Music Week and Dove Awards Program.

Truett talks with Gloria and Bill Gaither *(r)* of the Bill Gaither Trio. Chick-fil-A is the title sponsor of many concerts and the first and lead sponsor of Bill's Jubilaté New Year's Eve concert held in Atlanta each year.

It's a good life. Truett and Jeannette *(seated in rockers)* thank God for their children and grandchildren, the Whites and the Cathys, and friends, the Faulks.

A Don Cathy, *B* Cindy Cathy, *C* Seth Cathy, *D* David White, *E* John White, *F* Trudy White, *G* Rae Faulk, *H* Woody Faulk, *I* Rhonda Cathy, *J* Dan Cathy, *K* James Cathy, *L* Rachel Cathy, *M* Truett Cathy, *N* Angela White, *O* Joy White, *P* Jeannette Cathy, *Q* Andrew Cathy, *R* Mark Cathy, *S* John White IV, *T* Ross Cathy you'll be home. Afterward, I'll expect you to return the keys."

Prior to Dan's eighteenth birthday, we went automobile shopping at the various dealers throughout Atlanta. Dan decided on a Pontiac Firebird with four in the floor and loaded with extras.

We placed an order for the Firebird, customized to Dan's specifications. We all eagerly awaited the arrival of the auto and Dan's birthday.

In the meantime, I had a nameplate made that I had fastened to the dashboard. When I presented the car and handed Dan the keys, he walked around it, admiring it with great pride. He opened the door and immediately saw the nameplate on the dash. It read:

Custom made for DAN CATHY
Matthew 6:33

"What's Matthew 6:33, Dad?" Dan asked.

"Get your Bible and see."

Dan ran into the house and looked up the verse: "But seek ye first the kingdom of God, and his righteousness; and all these things shall be added unto you" (KJV).

I wanted Dan to receive the message that God had many blessings in store for him, materially and spiritually, if he would remember to seek God's guidance in every decision he made. I also wanted Dan to accept and respect the automobile as a gift from his heavenly Father channeled through his earthly father.

Fourteen months later, Bubba and I went automobile shopping. Because we had our original restaurant across from the Ford assembly plant, the manager, S. K. Cannon, invited us over to view the cars on the assembly line as well as hundreds in the parking lot. Right there Bubba decided on a Ford Gran Torino Sport and added that he wanted four in the floor, loaded with extras. We placed the order and waited for his eighteenth birthday.

Shortly before delivery date, Bubba asked, "Dad, are you going to get me a nameplate for my Ford?"

"I hadn't thought about it, Bubba, but if you would like to have one, of course, I'll put one in."

A big smile appeared on his face, and from his pocket he took out a piece of paper all rolled up. He handed me the verse he wanted—Deuteronomy 6:5: "And thou shalt love the LORD thy God with all thine heart, and with all thy soul, and with all thy might" (KJV).

He had chosen the greatest of the commandments. A flood of joy swept through me because my almost-eighteen-year-old son requested such words to be placed on his auto. There are things that have great value, yet they cannot be bought with dollars.

Twenty months later, Trudy approached me. "Daddy, isn't it time we talked about a car for me?"

"Not you, too, Trudy!" I exclaimed. I hadn't thought about her needing an automobile. "I was expecting someone else to furnish you with transportation."

"Daddy, you promised that when we reached eighteen. . . ."

I knew I was beaten. "Trudy, if I led you to believe that you would be included, I certainly will get you an auto, too."

Trudy selected a Ford Mustang with white interior and exterior, but she wanted an automatic transmission. And like the boys, she wanted the car loaded with extras.

Trudy didn't surprise me when she presented the verse she wanted on her nameplate—Luke 1:37: "For with God nothing shall be impossible" (KJV).

I can honestly say that Jeannette and I had not one concern about where those automobiles went or the conduct that took place inside them. We had no reason to. The nameplates often became conversation pieces for our children and their friends who rode with them.

Eighteen years have now passed since I presented Dan with his Pontiac. He still has that car. I think he considers it somewhat of a trophy. I know he believes in the importance of Matthew 6:33.

When they reached high school, the boys decided to go out for wrestling. I supported them in their decision. At the beginning of the school year as they stayed after school, practiced, and kept on practicing, often they didn't finish until seven, sometimes eight. I drove from our offices to pick them up, and they would come out, half-dressed, tired, and worn.

"That Coach Stallings nearly killed us tonight," Bubba would say.

"The same things over and over and over and over," Dan would add. "He's too rough and too demanding."

More than once, Dan worked out to the point of exhaustion. My son didn't realize how it upset me, but the coach assured me I had nothing to worry about.

"Dad, I want to quit the wrestling team," Bubba must have said every other day.

"Me, too," Dan would add. "It's not worth it."

"That is up to you boys," I told them. "It wasn't my idea for you to go out for wrestling, so you can quit if you want."

The conversation went on like that most of the way home. But the next day, both boys showed up for wrestling and went through the same hard discipline of Coach Johnny Stallings.

Then the real wrestling season started. Bubba, at the end of tenth grade, had twenty-two competitive matches (he was listed in the ninety-five-pound category), and he never lost any. That year he became the state wrestling champion for his weight.

Dan, a year ahead of Bubba in school, did not go out for wrestling until the season after Bubba started. Two years after Bubba's championship, Dan emerged. On his final match he won by a split-second takedown. When the referee declared Dan the winner, Bubba was standing at the edge of the mat, crying with his brother over the victory. He had become so emotionally involved with Dan's match that it might just as easily have been his own. I'll have to admit that Jeannette and I were crying, too.

The boys have since told me that during their high-school days at Woodward Academy, in College Park, Georgia, Coach Stallings influenced them more than any other teacher because he made demands of them. "I'm training you to be winners," he told his boys. I understand that Coach Johnny Stallings produced more wrestling champions than any other coach in the state.

Bubba had done well in wrestling and considered going for a scholarship and making wrestling the center of his college career. Previously both he and Dan had attended a special camp for wrestlers in Bethlehem, Pennsylvania, at Lehigh University.

Bubba came to talk it over with me. He wanted to go for the national championship in wrestling. After giving me all the information, he wanted to know how I felt. As I listened to him speak, his obvious enthusiasm showed through.

I have tried to teach my children to make their own decisions. If I did a good job of it early in their lives, my influence would be strong enough to help them make the right choices as adults.

"I know I can do it, Dad. I know I can be national champion." The glow in Bubba's eyes convinced me that he meant every word he said. He knew his ability.

"Bubba, are you willing to pay the price?" I asked. "Is it worth the self-discipline? What about the dieting? Are you willing to go through all of that?"

Bubba thought about that. I didn't try to talk him out of it; I wanted him to make the decision. He constantly struggled with his weight, which could not exceed ninety-five pounds because of his class. That's not much for a growing teenager. On family trips, sometimes he and Dan stayed in the car when we stopped to eat. Neither wanted to fight the temptation to overeat when they saw food around them. Those wrestlers tortured their bodies in order to excel at the sport. In order to weigh in at the correct poundage, some of those athletes would resort to laxatives, fasts, and saunas to get off the extra pounds and qualify for the match.

One time Dan got into a dangerous state because he regimented himself so closely that he lost all his body fat. That meant unless he ate more, his body would live off its muscle tissue. Many of the wrestlers went on a twenty-four-hour fast so they would not disqualify themselves. From my perspective, they lived on the borderline of starvation.

"I don't doubt your ability, Bubba, but I want you to decide if what you're going to get out of this is worth the price you have to pay."

Bubba thought it through carefully. Finally he said, "No, I don't think it is."

I was proud of him for making a tough decision. And I believed he had made the right choice.

Around our house, we lived with what I called Truett's Rules:

1. It's better to demonstrate than to dictate. If you set the example, you won't need to set so many rules.
2. Fifty percent of the battle ends when you make up your mind.

There is a time to be firm with children and a time to be lenient. It takes wisdom to know the difference. If I acted too firmly, I could ruin a relationship. Many times I thought of my father. When he said no or yes, he became adamant and would not change; his word was final. I determined I would learn to give in when it was a matter of major concern.

All three of our children grew up around Chick-fil-A. As the business expanded and as they grew older, they knew about the progress. They knew most of it from what we term hands-on experience; they put their hands to work in the restaurants. I wanted them treated like all the other employees. If anything, I may have put too much pressure on them, making them feel at times as if I expected too much from them.

Dan worked often at Chick-fil-A during high school and college and full-time during his summers, and his brother did the same. After his graduation from Georgia Southern in Statesboro, Dan came on the staff to a position in operations because I needed him badly. I had provided the product and the company to sell it, but I needed good people to take on leadership in areas I knew little about.

When Bubba finished college, he said, "Dad, I don't want to do the same as Dan. I want to learn the business from the ground floor."

That's exactly what he did. He became a carpenter's helper in the design and construction department under Perry Ragsdale. For eight months he worked for a carpenter and learned the hard things about constructing a Chick-fil-A restaurant.

Bubba later became the Operator of a Chick-fil-A Unit at Atlanta's Southlake Mall. He did as fine a job as anyone we've staffed anywhere. He currently functions as vice president of development with special responsibilities for the Dwarf House restaurants.

Trudy followed the example of her brothers by working at Chick-fil-A restaurants during high school and after she started college. She attended Samford University in Birmingham. Bubba graduated from Samford after one year at Furman University, Greenville, South Carolina. He worked part-time at our Chick-fil-A restaurant in Birmingham at Brookwood Village. He became good friends with another college student and part-time employee, John White, a special individual indeed as you'll see later.

At the end of Trudy's first year of college, we talked of the Chick-fil-A business. We would soon open a second Unit in Birmingham at the Century Plaza.

"Daddy, who is going to operate the new store in Birmingham?" Trudy asked.

"How about you operating it, Trudy? You could get a four-year education in one year. Save you a lot of time."

"What do you mean?"

"You open and operate the new restaurant at the Century Plaza, and you'll get the equivalent of a full college education in that first year."

"Do you really mean I could, Daddy?"

"I was only kidding you," I said, and I was.

"Well, I'm not kidding! I'd really like to do that."

"I'm not sure. . . ."

"You don't think I can do it, is that it?"

"Trudy, I hadn't thought you. . . ."

"I know as much about Chick-fil-A as Dan and Bubba. I've worked every summer and after school, haven't I?"

"Yes, but. . . ."

I spent the next half hour trying to talk my daughter out of her enthusiastic desire to operate the restaurant.

"I can do it, Daddy," she said.

She had planned to travel that summer with her college roommate, Leslie Parkman, to visit the girl's missionary parents in the Philippines and then go on around the world. "You'd have to forfeit your trip," I said, knowing she had looked forward to going. "Besides, Mr. Parkman has already worked out your itinerary."

"I'd still like to operate the restaurant."

The firmness in her voice convinced me. I know when I'm licked. "Okay, Trudy, you start training as soon as possible. Your restaurant opens in the fall."

At that time we had no training facilities or program. Operator-appointees worked under a competent Operator until they were ready to open their own restaurant.

I had told Trudy she would get four years' education in one year. I was wrong—she got it in six months . . . and made top marks. Both Bubba and John White went to work for her. John earned both a law degree and a master's degree in business. From my perspective, even more significant was the fact that he married my daughter in 1977.

Trudy, like the boys, had been taught to make her own decisions. Later I wished I hadn't taught her so well. When she took over the restaurant, she never called home for help or to ask, "Daddy, what should I do now?" I admired her independence, but I also worried a little.

One evening at home I was thinking about her. It was almost nine o'clock, and I knew she would be closing, so I phoned. "How has it gone today, Trudy?"

As soon as I asked that question, her voice broke. "You shouldn't have asked, Dad." She started crying.

There I was, 150 miles away, and my baby girl was crying her eyes out. "What's happening?" I finally broke in.

"Our Henny Penny cooker (the cooker we use to cook the Chick-fil-A products) hasn't been working. I called Morris Jackson at the Brookwood Village restaurant because I knew he had an extra fryer they weren't using and I've been cooking chicken all day in the french fryer."

I couldn't understand why she was upset. She seemed to have solved her problem.

But Trudy continued, "I sent John and Bubba over to get it for me. They went in a borrowed pickup." She described what happened. The top-heavy Henny Penny cooker stands about forty-eight inches high and fifteen inches wide. The boys put the fryer in the back of the pickup and started to drive away. They heard a terrible crash. The fryer had toppled over and fallen onto the asphalt. They stopped, picked up the pieces, and took it to Trudy's restaurant.

"I don't know what to do," Trudy wailed. "They brought in this messed-up Henny Penny cooker, and it doesn't work." She went into a fresh crying spell.

Keeping my voice as calm as I could, I said, "Trudy, the first thing in the morning, call somebody and have it repaired."

"But who knows how to repair something like that?"

"Call the power company. If they can't do it, they'll know who to call. Ask them to come by first thing in the morning."

Then Trudy calmed down and took hold of the situation. "You know, Dad, a man from the power company came by yesterday and ate here. He left his card and told me to give him a call if I ever needed any help."

"Trudy, now is the time you need him. Call him."

"Now? At nine o'clock?"

"Why not?" I said, sensing she needed a little push.

After hanging up, Trudy called the man's home. His wife answered and listened to Trudy's story. "I'm sorry, but he's not home now. He's at the bowling alley. Why don't you call him over there?"

"But I don't want to interrupt his game."

"He won't mind," the wife assured Trudy. "And it'll be very late when he gets in."

Trudy called and had him paged. He listened to her story.

"I'll send someone over the first thing in the morning," he said. "I'm not sure of my own schedule, but if I can make it, I'll be there, too."

He was as good as his word. By 9:00 A.M., a repairman arrived, figured out the problem, and told her what parts she needed to replace. He even told her where to order the parts.

Trudy called me after they left. She had her fryer working by noon that day. "Daddy, I don't know what I would have done if you hadn't called."

"Trudy," I said, "if you have a problem, you call. Other Operators call me when they need help. Besides, if operating a restaurant only meant opening the doors and depositing money in the bank, you'd have no challenge. I said you'd get a college education out of your experiences."

I also told her, as I suppose I've done dozens of times before and since, "Every problem has a solution. You just have to figure it out and then decide what to do."

During that year, she, along with other Operators, had to pick an Employee of the Year. She selected John White. Trudy, later Mrs. John White, took a lot of kidding over that choice.

John came to work in our corporate headquarters in the legal department. For the next three years, he was efficient and valuable as an employee as well as warm and responsible as a family member. John worked hard and won the respect of the others on the staff, which justified our decision to hire him. It really pleased me that all of my children were associated with Chick-fil-A. And all of them were doing it out of their choice to be part of the business.

In 1983, John and Trudy came by the house to tell Jeannette and me of a decision they had made. Their first words stunned us. As I listened to them speak, I thought of our children in their younger days. We had dedicated each of them to God. All three of them were following Jesus Christ, and all had married Christians.

All three of our children had invited Christ into their hearts and were baptized at the same time—Dan was ten; Bubba, nine; and Trudy, seven. They had matured together in their spiritual development, and it seemed the right time for each of them. Receiving Christ is a personal thing, and Jeannette and I felt this was a meaningful experience for each of them.

In those days we belonged to the Baptist church in Lovejoy. Pastor J. S. Brown talked to our children for a long time. Afterward he said, "They understand the gospel and believe in Jesus Christ. They're ready."

We consented and he baptized them and they joined the church. We remained active there for another five years. When our children approached their teen years, however, they wanted to go to another church.

"We love everybody at Lovejoy," the children said, "but the church is so small, they don't have much for us to do."

After much prayer and consideration, we moved

our membership to the First Baptist Church of Jones-boro, which offered an active program for teens and the whole family. The boys, along with their wives, are rais-ing their children in that church.

As I thought of Trudy, standing beside her brothers and waiting for immersion and later standing in front of the whole church and telling of her faith, tears came to my eyes. She had turned out to be a wonderful daughter, a fine Christian, a good wife, and a loving mother.

And now she was presenting to her parents some dramatic news.

"John and I are going to Brazil as missionaries."

Her words stung. Part of me kept thinking, *I ought to be happy about this. They want to serve the Lord more fully.* But the daddy in me couldn't respond that way. I thought of all the negative aspects of their going. We wouldn't see them for years. I was sixty-two years old then, and our grandchildren would grow up without us.

"Why do you want to go?" I asked, stalling for time, trying to think of a way to convince them to give up their plans.

"Because God directed us to go," Trudy said.

"I wish God had consulted your parents."

"Maybe He's telling you now, through us," John said quietly.

I didn't like their words, and for a long time, I couldn't get beyond my own sense of loss. This was my little girl, our baby.

Then I remembered reading somewhere that the Southern Baptists have a year's waiting period. When people apply to serve on the mission field, they sometimes do it in a moment of emotional excitement. They need time to think it over—and perhaps even change their minds. "Why don't you wait a year or so and give it plenty of thought?"

"Daddy, we've already waited a year," Trudy said.

She told us that in 1982 they had both felt strongly that they could serve God best as missionaries. They made a formal application to the mission board, but said nothing to anyone for a full year.

"We wanted to be sure," Trudy said. "We didn't want everyone to get all excited, then a year later say that we'd changed our minds. We've gone through the required waiting, Daddy, and we have no doubts about what we're supposed to do."

"I have some doubts," I managed to say. I could hardly believe what they were telling me, and I couldn't react logically. I had gotten so caught up in the idea of losing Trudy and John and their children, my grandchildren, that nothing else seemed to matter.

After they left that evening, I thought again of Trudy when she was growing up, and of her zeal. She was so much like Jeannette. She could talk to anybody and always seemed to be leading a group or speaking in the youth department at church.

I reminded myself that we had committed our children to God at their birth. That didn't make it any easier; I still didn't want them to go away.

They talked excitedly of their plans. After they attended an initial language school, John would be assigned to the position of treasurer, ministering to the needs of more than 350 Southern Baptist missionaries in South America. Both of them would also engage in evangelistic work. They talked about the things they would take with them, where they would live, the children's schooling. Everything had been decided.

"You know we'll do anything we can for you," I said, still grappling with the staggering news. "Trudy and John, why don't we commit this to God in prayer? Let's pray that if God wants you to go to Brazil, He'll make it clear and every door will open for you and. . . ."

"Keep praying," Trudy said. "But John and I feel convinced we've made the right decision."

All our children, including Trudy and John, had built homes nearby. Often during the next few days, I walked around the farm alone. I fed the cows and horses or rode the mower to cut the grass. Slowly I came to accept the fact of their going.

When they left the Atlanta airport headed for Brazil, tears filled my eyes, but I had accepted their leaving. I had progressed further and had even finally been able to say, "I'm proud of Trudy and John. They're going to South America to serve God."

Their leaving helped me to understand that we rear our children, teach them the best we can, then we have to release them. They have to make their own decisions and live their own lives.

In October 1984, Jeannette and I flew to Brazil and spent a week with them. They were still in language school, but we had time with them and the grandchildren. We prepared to leave on a Sunday evening. Trudy had wrapped Christmas presents, and by rearranging our suitcases, Jeannette and I could carry them back with us.

As I watched her put those presents into the suit-case, for the first time I realized that she would not be home for Christmas. That had never happened before. Tears filled my eyes, but I didn't say anything. I couldn't.

Trudy knows her dad pretty well. She stopped a minute and put her arms around me. "Dad, the only reason we can do this is that we feel it is in keeping with God's calling."

I have learned to accept that. But it hasn't been easy.

Today Dan is senior vice president of operations, and Bubba serves as vice president of development with special responsibilities for the expanding Dwarf House restaurants. My grandchildren enjoy coming to the farm to ride my trail bikes and roam the acreage. I think the little ones could say "motorcycle" before "Mama" and "Daddy," they love those wheels so much. It takes youth to keep up with youngsters. Jeannette and I like to tell people that we love our grandchildren twice as much: when they come and when they leave. God knew what He was doing when He gave children to young parents.

A few years ago, our two sons—then teenagers—and I were on a business trip to Houston, Texas, so we visited the Methodist church in that city pastored by our friend, Dr. Charles Allen. He had formerly served as pastor of Grace Methodist Church in Atlanta and now was the pastor of one of the largest Methodist churches in America.

Dr. Allen read from the pulpit a letter he had re-ceived just that week from a pastor friend in Georgia. The letter began:

Dear Charles:

This is the saddest letter I've ever written. We have just been notified by the authorities that our son has been picked up for armed robbery in Houston.

Would you check with the authorities and see if you could visit him? Assure him of our love and concern.

Dr. Allen said he dashed down to the police department but was told that the boy was actually picked up in California and would be back in Houston on Monday. That evening he phoned his pastor friend. During the conversation, the pastor's wife said, "Charles, next time you call, please don't call so late. You see, when the telephone rings late, we get all excited, thinking possibly it might be our son calling home."

"How long has it been since you heard from your son?" Dr. Allen asked his friends.

"The call from the FBI was the first call in five years with news about our son," they said.

As I sat there between my two young sons, I wondered, *Lord, could this ever happen to me?*

I came away from that meeting renewed by a commitment to be the kind of father to my children that God intended me to be. And each time I see the statistics in the newspapers, I'm made aware of how the trend is going. I feel that God did not call any of us to be a failure. A believer might be temporarily unable to meet established goals, but that person who does his best within the providence of God can never be considered a failure or a flop.

In 1900, the figures indicated that 1 out of 100 marriages ended in divorce. By 1920, 1 out of 20 ended in divorce, and by 1975, 1 marriage in 3 ended in divorce. In the statistics given to me just recently about the Atlanta metropolitan area, there are 16,500 marriages and 15,000 divorces in the course of a year.

In Clayton County where I live, there were 1,895 marriages this past year and 2,284 divorces—more divorces granted than marriages.

Out of thirty boys in my Sunday school class last year, one-third of them came from broken homes or had severe problems within the home.

Parents need to patch up their quarrels before they put their children to bed. Sometimes the adults are reconciled after the children are asleep, and the youngsters get up the next morning thinking that their parents are still angry with each other and might be planning to be divorced.

Few sentiments on the subject of success can match those in this poem about the responsibility of parenthood:

MASTER POTTER

This child whose life I touch with mine
    Is like a piece of clay;
I take his gentle will in hand,
    And shape it day by day.

If I regard that God is love,
    Then likely he will too,
Because this yielding piece of clay
    Will pattern things I do.

If I respect my fellowman
    And all his burdens share,
I'll find this young life being shaped
    To love and really care.

The turns upon the wheel will shape
    His habits, good and bad;
The edges rough and smooth are mine,
    Upon this growing lad.

So thou who art the potter great,
    Mold my life day by day;
That I, in turn, may shape this child
    Whose life is trusting clay.*

*Muriel Blackwell, *Potter and Clay* (Nashville: Broadman Press, 1975).

8

A BRAINSTORM
CALLED CHICK-FIL-A

Ideas come from God. They are pleasant and exciting, but they won't keep. They have to be acted on.

During the months after the fire when I was managing only my original restaurant, the Dwarf House in Hapeville, I was on the verge of the greatest business idea of my life. It would present a challenge far more demanding than anything I had undertaken.

The chicken entrees on our menu intrigued me. I began to experiment with various kinds of orders: chicken steak sandwich . . . leg and thigh . . . chicken salad. . . .

Poultry has several positive factors. It is less fattening, more nutritious, and more economical than beef, and it is popular with customers. We wanted to keep chicken on the Dwarf House menu, but chicken orders slowed down our flow of service.

My mother served chicken in our boarding house. I recalled that the white breast meat was always the most popular at the table, a delicacy that I was not able to taste very often because we children ate what was left over—wings . . . necks . . . the back . . . and even the feet. Chicken feet are good, especially if that's all you have. The toenails are a little tough, though. If you have hot biscuits and gravy, they're super delicious.

One day I removed the bone and skin from the chicken breast and found that the cooking time was cut in half whether the meat was panfried or deep-fat fried. I next discovered that the breast did not need to be cooked as long as the other parts of the chicken.

As an experiment, I placed the breast inside a buttered bun and served it as a sandwich. This eliminated the greasy fingers often associated with eating chicken and made the sandwich a meal in itself, which it is. The idea was simple enough, but next came the testing of the seasoning and seasoned coating, the pickles to give the sandwich character, the change from ordinary cooking oil to the more nutritious peanut oil in which to cook it, and the serving of it on a toasted, buttered bun.

I tried one mixture of seasonings after another, always asking my customers how it tasted. "I want your honest opinion," I told them.

I would get mixed reviews. Some would even ask, "What is it, quail?" When my tasters no longer offered suggestions on how to make it better, I decided that I had found the perfect combination and that I should stick with it.

As I moved closer to the finished recipe, I developed a fryer to speed up cooking. My first apparatus was an automatic fryer with a timer, one that also lifted the chicken out of the fry kettle. But the process took too long. Then I recalled how my mother had cooked chicken in an iron skillet with a lid and served it to our boarders. I tried the lid idea. It held the steam inside, speeded up the cooking, and left the chicken juicier.

✳ ————————————————

*We make a living
by what we get . . .
But we make a life
by what we give.*

Author Unknown

————————————————

At about this time, food equipment manufacturers introduced pressure fryers. Although my improvised cooker did the job, the new pressure cookers did it better. Now I could standardize the product and pressure-cook my chicken from start to finish in four minutes—about the same time as hamburgers—while sealing in the moisture and eliminating a greasy taste. We no longer had to prepare chicken in advance; we had no cooked chicken left over; our sandwich could be served piping hot without delaying the customers.

From the beginning, sales boomed. How could I best promote the new product? I thought of billboards, radio ads, newspaper display ads, and direct mail. After giving the matter a great deal of thought, I decided to start with newspaper ads.

At that time, Tony Grey and Jack Troy each owned struggling weekly newspapers in Forest Park. Besides being business rivals, they had deep personal differences that showed up in their editorials as each sharply criticized the other.

I phoned each man and made the same offer, "How would you like to have a full-page ad in your paper?" Each responded enthusiastically, of course, so I said, "Come to the Dwarf House at two o'clock tomorrow afternoon and bring your photographer with you."

Both editors showed up right on time. When they saw each other, they realized that I had manipulated them.

"What's going on, Truett?" Jack said, obviously ignoring Tony.

"You promised me a full-page ad," Tony reminded me. "But I didn't know about anyone else being here."

"I'll tell you two something," I said. "I'll give you each a full-page ad if you'll do one thing for me."

Tony eyed Jack and asked, "What's the 'one thing'?"

"Sit over there," I said, nodding toward the circle booth. "Eat one of my chicken sandwiches, and let your photographers take a picture of you two shaking hands."

They stared at me, not sure what was coming next. I continued, "Then, I want you to put the picture in both newspapers. I've even got the caption: 'We disagree on many things, but this is one thing we agree on—this is the *best* chicken sandwich that we've ever eaten.' How about it?"

Tony Grey burst into laughter, enjoying the humor of the situation and the fact that I had conned both of them into coming. Jack Troy froze. He didn't say anything, but I could figure out what was going on in his head. He didn't know if he wanted to shake hands with Tony. At the same time, he needed the income for a full-page ad. Economics won. He nodded and said, "All right."

When that photograph appeared in both papers, it accomplished all that I had hoped for. It became the talk of the community. People kept asking, "How in the world did you manage to get those two fellows to agree on anything?"

I didn't tell them that both men wanted the ad. I let them think of me as a great peacemaker. I also continued to give both papers ads for my chicken sandwich.

On April 10, 1983, Dr. Robert Schuller invited me to tell that story on his Sunday morning television program, "The Hour of Power," and later he put the story into his book *The Be (Happy) Attitudes.* "Blessed are the peacemakers," he wrote. "In S. Truett Cathy's humorous anecdote, of course, the two editors were just peace *talkers!* What we want to learn to be today is true peace-*makers.*"

Sales for the new sandwich continued to climb. Eventually it outsold hamburgers at the Dwarf House. That caused me to think ahead. I had no intention of starting a chain of restaurants. The Forest Park experience had cured me of that idea. I didn't want to go through that again.

Then I had an idea: Why not create a trade name with a logo and promote just the chicken sandwich? I presented my idea to Jeannette. We talked about it, and I asked our friends for their opinions. Everyone agreed that the idea was a good one.

A patent attorney informed me, "You can't register a dictionary word. You need to misspell it, turn it upside down, or do something to distinguish the name."

As I was driving home, I took the words *chick* and *fillet* and hit upon the name Chick-fil-A. I especially liked the *A* at the end. It reminded me of top quality, sanitary conditions, and excellent service. It's a little bit tricky. Some people pronounce it "Chick-a-filla," "Chick-a-fill," "Chick Buffet," "Chevrolet," and other terms as their attempts at a bit of humor.

Through a friend, I contacted the talented people at the Richard Heiman Company and asked for their help in creating the art for a logo. In our first conversation, Richard warned me, "Only one product in ninety stays on the market longer than five years."

That was a scary thought, especially since I would

be investing so much money in the logo and initial advertising of the concept. I thought about the odds against me. "I believe in my chicken sandwich," I said. That faith gave me the determination to go ahead.

By 1964, I was ready to begin promoting my product. I rented an office a block away from the Dwarf House and hired my first Chick-fil-A employee, Brooksie Kirk, who has been my personal secretary ever since then. In those days, Brooksie did everything from handling the correspondence and filing to serving as lunch-time cashier at the Dwarf House if I was held up in town.

I began my first promotional efforts for Chick-fil-A to other restaurateurs as a licensed item to add to their menus. Brooksie, Jeannette, and I cooked and served free samples of Chick-fil-A at the Southeastern Restaurant Trade Show. Ours became the most popular booth at the show. Since we provided free food, the workers and booth attenders came to our booth to eat. All were impressed and gave a strong positive vote to Chick-fil-A.

By the end of the show, I had plenty of prospects, mostly from independent restaurants. Within four months nearly fifty restaurants had added the Chick-fil-A sandwich to their menus.

The Goode Brothers Poultry Company provided me with deboned chicken breasts. They also applied my special seasonings formula and packed the chicken in five-pound boxes. Lewis Grizzard, a columnist for the *Atlanta Journal & Constitution,* joked that my formula for seasonings was "buried in a box that has been hidden in gorilla Willie B.'s cage at the Atlanta Zoo."

I arranged with a local restaurant supply house to sell equipment to each place that served the Chick-fil-A product under my trade name. I could now reproduce my chicken sandwich anywhere in the country.

During that early period, the decision makers at McDonald's expressed an interest in my product. I didn't push hard. I was actually afraid that they or another fast-food chain would take my idea, change it enough so that they didn't violate any laws, and sell it through their chain. But McDonald's didn't buy into Chick-fil-A, and fortunately for me, none of those chains woke up to the idea until some fifteen years later when Chick-fil-A was generating annual sales in excess of $100 million. Today, chicken has become a $2 billion segment within the more than $60 billion fast-food industry.

In 1967, we dedicated the first Chick-fil-A Unit. It was squeezed into a little patched-up cubbyhole of Atlanta's Greenbriar Mall, the Southeast's first enclosed regional shopping center. We had 384 square feet of space at Greenbriar, an area approximately 13 by 30 feet. After two decades, that original Unit has been enlarged and continues to show good sales and profits.

We built the menu around a few basics: the boneless breast chicken sandwich, potato fries, coleslaw, and lemon pie and lemonade made daily from freshly squeezed lemons. Added later were Chick-fil-A Nuggets,® chicken salad, and hearty breast of chicken soup. The Chick-fil-A Nuggets® were the first of the popular nugget products to be sold nationally by a major fast-food chain.

Four years after perfecting and testing the sandwich creation, I established four tenets by which our company would be run:

1. The company would not sell franchises but would form joint ventures with independent Operators.
2. Chick-fil-A would build in only major shopping malls.
3. Future growth would be financed mainly from within.
4. The chief emphasis would be on people.

The first guarantees quality, supervision, and the motivation of partnership. The second was timely in 1967 when enclosed shopping malls were becoming popular. The third decision brought slow but certain early growth and enabled expansion. The fourth is the essence of the philosophy of life that God has entrusted to us.

Promotional slogans in the past have included these: "No Bones About It," "Beware, Chick-fil-A is habit forming," and "First 'n' Best." The current one is: "Taste It. You'll Love It For Good.®"

The small and the great have sampled our proud bird. During President Lyndon Johnson's 1967 presidential campaign, his wife, Lady Byrd, was planning a speaking tour through Georgia. When I learned that Betty Talmadge (wife of Senator Herman Talmadge) had arranged to have her famous ham served at a luncheon for the First Lady, I called the senator and asked if we could not also serve her a Chick-fil-A sandwich, especially since Georgia was known as a poultry state.

"Come on over for lunch," the senator replied, "and bring some of your sandwiches with you."

He liked them and immediately contacted Lady Byrd's secretary to arrange the luncheon. Unfortunately, her appearance was to be in Savannah instead of Atlanta. That didn't stop us, though. Jeannette and I rented a small pressure fryer, took all the fixin's for the chicken, coleslaw, and potato salad, and drove down. An official photographer had trouble getting to the scene on time, but a photo snapped by the state trooper who escorted us to the First Lady's luncheon turned out just fine and was suitable for use in the local newspaper. So we gathered some publicity from our hard work after all.

Each year Chick-fil-A brings all of our Operators and their spouses together for a business seminar in an exotic resort complex. The event now costs the company more than $1 million, but it is money well spent. At those seminars we listen to sales experts, psychologists, our pastoral advisor, Dr. Charles Carter of the First Baptist Church of Jonesboro where my wife and I attend, and various inspirational speakers. At our annual seminar, we give away Mark VII Lincoln Continentals in Chick-fil-A's "Symbol of Success" program. Through this program, we give a new Lincoln to an Operator to use for one year if sales in his or her Unit increase by 40 percent or more in one year. If that Operator shows at least a 40 percent increase the second year, he or she gets the title to the car. More than a hundred and ten Operators have reached this goal since 1975. If they don't reach the 40 percent in the second year, the Operators may purchase the car at half price. We awarded forty-six in 1984 alone. Other incentive awards for Operators include trips, merchandise, and cash bonuses.

Free samples of our chicken products are offered to passersby at the various Units in shopping malls throughout the country as our number one marketing technique. We tell them, "It's a boneless, skinless breast of chicken served on a piping hot buttered bun with a kosher dill chip." Between the fillets and the Nuggets® our restaurants typically sample some 3,550 pounds per Unit annually.

I made it a habit to be present at the opening dedication ceremony for each new Unit. Occasionally I'd try to give a hand the following day as well. One day a Unit ran out of our Icedream mix so I rushed to the kitchen refrigerator, returned with a new container of mix, and dumped it into the hopper. Only too late did I realize that I had just poured coleslaw dressing into the Icedream machine. That put us out of the popular Chick-fil-A Icedream business for a while and required a thorough cleaning.

It's easy to apply for a position as an Operator of a Chick-fil-A Unit but hard to qualify. Our Human Resources Department spends a lot of time investigating the applicants, even though it is rather easy to size up an individual in the first two minutes. If the shoes are not shined, the handshake is not firm, the hair is not groomed—these are indications that the person does not give proper attention to personal matters. To manage people, you must first be able to manage your personal life.

We note how a person treats his family, if he's

happy and well adjusted, and if he has a history of stable employment. We don't select or even seriously consider an Operator or a member of the staff unless we want the individual to be with us until one of us retires or dies. Because of that, Chick-fil-A has one of the lowest turnover rates in the restaurant industry. For Operators, it's less than 6 percent a year. Our crew members, about fifteen thousand young people, have a turnover rate of less than 25 percent that of the fast-food industry.

I picked up the phone one day to take a call from an applicant. The first words I heard were, "What the ——— has happened to my resume?" I could tell him what was going to happen to it real quick if nothing had happened to it so far.

We stress the need for education, but there are exceptions—like Red Witten. At the age of nineteen, he was employed at one of our Units in the Tidewater area of Virginia. The Operator said that every time he returned from several days away, Red would have the Unit spic-and-span, the stockroom tidy, and the rest rooms spotless.

Another Chick-fil-A Unit across the bay had been open for two years but had never made any money. The Operator suggested that we give the Unit to Red to see what he could do. "He just might accept the challenge," he said.

We hated to take Red out of college, but with one year under his belt, he knew more than many people did who had completed all four years. He joyously accepted the offer.

The very first month under Red's management, that Unit showed a profit. Red had the desire to please and the desire to do his job better than anyone else. That Unit started to grow. Its sales jumped 58 percent that first year, qualifying Red, at that time, for a Mark V Lincoln in the Symbol of Success sales incentive program.

By then, he was twenty years old and engaged to be married. He wanted earnestly to purchase a house to which he could take his bride. One evening after work, he got into his car and prayed that the Lord would guide him to the right house. He took another way home that evening and saw a cute little house for sale. An elderly Christian couple owned it, and they agreed to financial terms Red could handle.

That year he brought his fiancée to the annual seminar. Together they drove home in their new Lincoln. I went to their wedding, and Red took me to see their house. He had set up a shop and had made some of their furniture. Where the rooms were bare, he had the oak flooring gleaming with wax.

A person succeeds or fails according to the multitude of decisions that are made day after day. The right decisions lead to rewards; incorrect decisions lead to disappointment and delay.

Chick-fil-A gives a $1,000 college scholarship to a restaurant employee who has worked for two years, has averaged working twenty hours a week, and is recommended by the Operator. This scholarship program was started in 1973 and assists the student in meeting the financial obligations of college and it looks good on that young person's resume when the graduate goes looking for employment. Chick-fil-A restaurants have given more than $5 million to crew members in these $1,000-scholarships.

New Units are built from the profits of Chick-fil-A. We try not to go into debt to expand, although we have occasionally done so in the past. A typical expansion finds Chick-fil-A negotiating a lease while a mall is being built. We then design and build a restaurant (about 1,800 square feet) and furnish it for about $250,000. An Operator is selected who then subleases the restaurant and puts up a refundable deposit of $5,000. Once the restaurant opens, the Operator pays himself a draw of $20,000 per year, returns 15 percent of sales to Chick-fil-A, Inc., as a service charge, then splits the restaurant's net figure fifty-fifty with Chick-fil-A.

Retired people often apply. Some say to me, "You know, those Chick-fil-A Units look like something I could manage quite well. They seem to be run so easily."

The mark of professionalism is taking a difficult job and making it look easy. Because of the extensive training of our restaurant staff, it *does* look easy. But actually, there can be a lot of headaches behind the scene. If Suzie doesn't show up for work and the pressure fryer isn't working and sales are down and the mall is undergoing renovation and. . . .

Planning ahead is the key. You have to anticipate your needs. For example, you are going to need more workers this Saturday because of heavy advertising of sales by the major department stores in the mall. It's a challenge. You are always trying to outguess the public.

If an Operator wishes to cancel his agreement, the $5,000 deposit is refundable, but as I've noted, the turnover rate of those who quit is less than 6 percent. Two requirements of being an Operator are that the Operator run only one restaurant and must be on-site to manage it.

For the $5,000 deposit, the Operator gets a trademark, a fully-stocked restaurant to operate, advertising assistance, and four weeks of training at our Atlanta corporate headquarters and a fifth week of field training with all expenses paid. This includes classroom training, on-the-job experience, and instruction in how to manage a crew as well as carry out company policy. Operators are expected to participate financially in a national advertising program run three to four times a year, placing local newspaper, radio and, in some areas, TV ads.

It's up to the Operator to control costs, increase sales, and generate profits. But a capable Operator is unlimited in realizing potential income, ranging from $20,000 to nearly $200,000 annually. Location is important, but more essential than location is the ability of the Operator to manage well and to attract good employees. We do all we can to make our Operators successful because if they're successful, so is the company.

Ten free-standing Chick-fil-A restaurants have been built in the Atlanta area as of 1988. "Free-standing" means they are outside a mall. We expect to expand these nationwide in time. An extended breakfast menu is being offered in addition to a typical menu of Chick-fil-A items. The growing demand for Chick-fil-A products prompts us to look at the free-standing concept as a way to serve more customers more often.

Sometimes people remind me, "It's nothing so great to take the bone out of a chicken breast and put it into a bun."

"I know that," I reply. "That's why I was able to do it."

Think how those hours spent testing the spices for the seasoning and coater . . . experimenting with cooking . . . changing the oil type to peanut oil . . . paid off. Just 5 percent more effort turned into 100 percent more success. It's always too soon to quit, and it's always easier to succeed at what you've started than to quit early and fail.

MOVIN' ON

CHORUS:
Chick-fil-A we're movin' on.
Chick-fil-A we're growin' strong.
We're one big happy family,
That's the way at Chick-fil-A.

We are strong hand in hand.
We are happy side by side.
Our hearts are joined together,
By a sense of family pride.
Every day is an adventure,
When you're striving for a goal.
There's a spirit of excitement,
When we see the dream unfold.

CHORUS

It's so fun to make our living,
Doing what we love to do.
When you're working with your friends,
Every day is fresh and new.
We're exploring new horizons.
Reaching, striving every day.
And the way we work together,
Is the pride of Chick-fil-A.

CHORUS

CHORUS

CHORUS

We're one big happy family.
That's the way at Chick-fil-A.

TASTE IT.
YOU'LL LOVE IT FOR GOOD.®

9

A DEDICATION

W*hen each new Unit is opened, a dedication dinner just before a grand opening draws together the Operator, new employees (80 percent young people), opening crew (Operators and experienced employees from other nearby Units), home office staff people, and special guests. Following is a message by the author at the opening of a Chick-fil-A Unit at Cutler Ridge Mall, south Florida:*

We are pleased to welcome you all to this grand occasion. Perry Ragsdale, vice president of design and construction, came to me three months ago and said, "Well, it looks as though everything is going according to schedule except for the Unit down there at Cutler Ridge. This one is going to be tight."

But here we are, ready to open on schedule tomorrow morning. It's important to open these Units to coincide with the opening of the mall that hosts them. We don't pick these dates. If they overlap with other openings, we just have to make it.

Completing a Unit in five weeks is close to a record. Everything was a challenge, but we are happy for the way our staff met those challenges.

Chick-fil-A operates in a different way from just about any other business. We try to base our principles on Scripture, and it works. Jesus told us to treat the other fellow as we would like to be treated. That just about wraps up our attitude toward the people we will be serving. The customer is always king. He or she is always right.

You know the kind of service you like to have from people behind a counter. That's the kind of service we want you to offer to the customers.

You are going to determine whether this Unit is successful or not. Chick-fil-A here at Cutler Ridge Mall will be as successful as our employees permit it to be.

There's an old saying around the office, "The Unit Operator attracts the kind of people that he deserves to have. If he deserves to have lousy employees, he *gets* lousy employees; if he deserves *good* people, he attracts good people."

We screen very carefully our Unit Operators. Therefore, we assign our unit realizing that this is the most important decision we can make. We can decorate it beautifully and put the best equipment in there and prepare the very best food, but if we don't have the very best Operator, we have blown the whole thing.

We spend many days evaluating this matter. We are placing our reputation and our future in the hands of one individual. Because we build the Unit and then lease it to the Operator, the ability and the character of the individual are more important than his money.

Bob Gager will operate this unit as an independent Operator. You will work for him rather than for Chick-fil-A. You will be working for Chick-fil-A Cutler Ridge.

I want you folks to know how fortunate you are to work for a person like Bob. We know a lot about Bob. He worked as the manager of a men's store at the

✳ _____

*It's always easier
to dismiss a person
than to train him.
No great leader ever
built a reputation
on firing people.*

_____

Southlake Mall in Atlanta. Jimmy Collins, our executive vice president, buys his suits there. Bob always made a special effort to fit Jimmy right with the kind of suit he liked. Sometimes he'd have a dozen suits brought in from other locations just for Jimmy to try on to see if he liked any of them. There was no obligation whatever.

Jimmy planted the seed of a thought in Bob's mind one day when he asked, "Have you ever thought about making a career of Chick-fil-A?"

"Well," Bob replied, "we've thought about it, but we never did feel we could afford to get involved."

So Jimmy explained briefly how a person could get involved with the company. Bob came to the headquarters office as quickly as he could. He was eager to locate in the Miami area with his parents and other relatives. Cathy, his wife, was eager to get down here as well. This unit was designed just for them.

The same principles that work in a men's clothing store work in a food operation. He's been in training. By now, we hope he knows how to cook chicken, how to make coleslaw, and how to put meringue on a lemon pie. Basically he's got all of the things we look for in an Operator, one who is going to represent us well.

Let me give you something to think about, the truth of which becomes more clear to me as I get older. It takes time to succeed, and it takes time to fail; but it takes more time to fail than it does to succeed. Do you agree?

I was brought up to believe that if you were going to succeed, you would have to pay a price. There is a price to be paid, but in the long run you'll find that it takes less time to do a thing right than to do it wrong.

The rewards are so much greater. The things you want to accomplish in life *can* be accomplished if you do them and do them right.

How many here in this room want to be successful? Are there any here who purposely want to make flops of themselves?

Well, then, let's assume that everyone wants to be successful, whether it's washing dishes, digging ditches, or whatever. We want to help you in your efforts to be successful. We have a responsibility toward you to help you carry out some of the goals you have set for yourself.

This Chick-fil-A Unit is like a football team with Bob Gager as the coach. He is going to put strict demands on you, the players. If he's not a good coach, he's going to let you do just whatever you please. That's the easy way. But good coaches put great demands on their players in order to win the game.

I asked my friend, Bobby Richardson, the second baseman for the New York Yankees who played in more World Series games than any other player, "What is more important in winning a game—the players or the coach?" Bobby replied that he guessed the players were more important, but he added, "The coach had better be able to pick good players."

That's the way it is in business. The leader doesn't have to be a high performer if he's able to pick the players—the employees. He must first set the example, demonstrate rather than dictate, train his people, and motivate them. It's easy, but it takes the "want to" as well as the skills.

I was sitting in a meeting not long ago with six people. The man beside me headed up a large law firm. He was telling me how fortunate he thought he was in hiring a top law student just out of Emory University. This young man had graduated number two in his class. "But you know," my friend said, "we lost a couple of cases recently simply because this young man didn't show up in court at the proper time."

He said the young fellow would sometimes come to the office at nine, sometimes at nine-thirty or later. Sometimes he would spend half an hour for lunch, sometimes an hour and a half. "Put him in a library," he said, "and he's a whiz bang. But I don't know how long I can tolerate him because he doesn't understand the basic principles involved in performance."

My sons and I had the opportunity to visit Earl Nightingale in Chicago. He has made a lifelong study of what causes people to fail and what causes them to succeed. Mr. Nightingale came up with the evaluation that 90 percent of the people succeed simply because they have a good attitude and 10 percent succeed because they have some special ability or talents that the rest do not have.

These observations gave me encouragement because when I was in school, I never was an achiever. I wasn't able to make the chorus, I never could play a musical instrument, I didn't excel in sports, and I certainly didn't excel academically. But I had established some good work habits and had an attitude that has been very beneficial to me.

Coach Gager here will challenge you to be at your best at all times. He'll observe every move you make—particularly your relationship with the customer. If you haven't handled a situation professionally, it's his responsibility to call you over to the sidelines. He'll not embarrass you in front of other employees or customers, but he'll suggest a better way of handling the situation. He'll put you back on position, observe you further, and see if you caught on. If you didn't catch on, he'll take you aside again and repeat the instructions. If you still can't carry out his instructions and aren't performing at your best, you may be placed on the bench or dismissed from the team.

We are here tonight to get to know one another better at this dedication dinner. We want to honor God in all we do.

One day I took two thirteen-year-old boys from my Sunday school class to Oklahoma City. As we were straightening our ties and getting ready for the meeting, one of them asked, "Now, Mr. Cathy, who are we dedicating this place to?"

I said, "Well, Joe, we are going to dedicate it to the Lord."

He said, "Oh."

He had in mind the kind of dedication a disc jockey does for someone who has a birthday or an anniversary. But in this case, it's more a dedication of our selves than anything else. What we are saying is, "Lord, we thank You for bringing us this far. We ask You for direction. We are giving this Unit to You. We hope it will be successful, but we are not guaranteed that it will be. You may have some lessons for us to learn through disappointments."

Tonight we have with us Rev. Tom Watson to lead us in a prayer of dedication. Pastor, we feel that our food business is akin to yours, that of ministering to needs. Two things are central to life: physical food and spiritual food. Ours, too, is a divine business—that of providing physical food for physical needs.

We want to dedicate this Unit to the honor and glory of the Lord and ask His blessing on us. May this be an asset to Him in this area of ministry, and may we recognize Him from whom our strength and power come.

The concluding words are those spoken by Rev. Watson.

It is a privilege to come and dedicate a business. Here in south Florida we don't have too many businesses that are dedicated to the Lord.

I read recently in *U.S. News and World Report* an article stating that America is on the decline because of the decline of the Christian work ethic. The article talked about the early days in the not-too-long ago when there was a Christian work ethic, which said, "We owe the employer a day's work . . . we're supposed to be honest . . . we're supposed to do the job we are given." It's interesting to observe that a secular journal like the *U.S. News and World Report* made this point.

We hope that since we are dedicating this Unit to the Lord tonight, you will have a Christian work ethic and will demonstrate that every day you are on the job.

Let's have prayer:

Our Father, we are conscious that the Bible tells us that except the Lord build the house they labor in vain that build it. And although there are many houses that are seemingly successful as far as the business world is concerned, we recognize that they are built on sand and someday will crumble.

We are thankful that we can dedicate to You this business, along with the others that are to be built. Thank You for Christian concepts and for the young people who have wanted jobs allowing them to be in the Lord's house on the Lord's Day.

We pray that You will make them conscious that You have opened this for them and that it's an answer to their prayer and to our prayer.

We pray for Bob and Cathy. We know that there are so many, many difficult moments in getting a business started. There will be times when anxiety will be there and frustration will be there, and yet we pray that You will stand very close to them when the disappointments of business come. Help them to remember this night, this moment, when we have said, "Lord, we dedicate it to You."

We thank You for what we have seen and heard tonight. We thank You for the possibility of this being a real demonstration to a skeptical world that a business can operate on Christian principles.

And now, Lord, thank You again for the good time together, for the food, and for Your blessings. We pray in Christ's name, Amen.

10

GOD PRESENTS
MANY SURPRISES

I'm often asked, "What do Christian princi-
ples have to do with running a corporation?" My reply
is that they have everything to do with running Chick-
fil-A. Ours is only one company among many whose
honesty and integrity match biblical principles.

In the April 1987 issue, *Fortune* magazine's Associate Editor Edward C. Baig wrote an article titled "Prof-
iting with Help from Above." His article opens by
featuring our Monday morning devotional period at
Chick-fil-A headquarters.

"Hundreds of executives," Editor Baig noted, "run
their companies according to their interpretations of
God's laws." He noted with some amazement the commitment of many chief executive officers to the Bible
and how it affects their businesses. Included in *Fortune's* article was the story of J. McDonald Williams,
managing partner of Trammell Crow Co., the nation's
largest privately held real estate developer. Mr. Williams was quoted as saying he stops short of imposing
his religious views on company employees, but he
teaches a Sunday school class in his church and spends
time on the streets of Dallas with other local executives
to help feed the homeless.

Sanford McDonnell of McDonnell Douglas (1986 revenues: $12.6 billion) was once a "plain-vanilla Presbyterian." After coming to faith in Jesus Christ, he says the experience "gives me a peace that I did not have before."

Max De Press, chief executive of Herman Miller Office Furniture based in Zeeland, Michigan, finds that "the Book of Luke teaches me about leadership, . . . James teaches me about the work ethic, and the Apostle Paul about relationships."

Fred Roach, formerly president of General Development Corporation, now head of Centennial Homes, Inc., a real estate subsidiary of Weyerhaeuser Corporation, likes "to share the good news of Jesus Christ with others." But one of his purchasing agents wasn't impressed when Mr. Roach fired him.

"You can't do this," the offended employee said. "Jesus tells us to forgive seventy times seven."

"I'm not Jesus," Mr. Roach replied, "and you're still fired."

In its December 1, 1986, issue, *Forbes* magazine states, "Is religious commitment unusually strong in today's executive suites? Unmistakably so." According to a *Forbes* survey of the leaders of the nation's one hundred largest corporations, religious commitment is even stronger than in the general population. Of the respondents to the survey, 65 percent said that they and their families regularly attend church or synagogue. The attendance figure for the overall U.S. population is only about 40 percent.

Barbara Kallen, who wrote the article for *Forbes*, noted,

*———————————————

*If you
plant for days
—plant flowers.
If you
plant for years
—plant trees.
If you
plant for eternity
—plant ideas
and ideals into the
lives of others.*

———————————————

Among the 100 executives in our survey are a Sunday school teacher (Hays T. Watkins of CSX), a Baptist minister's son (Lennie S. Skaggs of American Stores) and a former seminarian honored by the Pope (Edward L. Hennessy Jr. of Allied-Signal). Until recently Laurence A. Tisch of Loews Corp. and CBS regularly brought a rabbi to his office to study Talmud. Says the Reverend Bowers of St. Bartholomew's, whose congregants include book publisher Charles Scribner, Bankers Trust Company President Charles S. Sanford Jr. and American Diversified Enterprises President Mar Haas, "I see more people interested in the Church than in a long time. Executives are coming in at 6:30 in the morning to study the Bible."*

Studies show that in addition to being more religious, the men at the top are more often still married to the wife of their youth.

Mr. Baig quoted me as getting "particular joy from making peace among quarreling employees in Chick-fil-A." That's true, and I try everything I know to foster goodwill among our corporate family. But when a person or an Operator is responsible for a $500,000 restaurant investment by Chick-fil-A and isn't doing anything with it, that person is not being a good steward of the Lord.

Other periodicals that have carried feature articles about Chick-fil-A include *Success, Entrepreneur, Income Opportunities, Inc., Decision* published by the Billy Graham Evangelistic Association, *Venture, Forbes,*

*Adapted by permission of *Forbes* magazine, December 1, 1986. © Forbes Inc., 1986.

Nation's Restaurant News, Restaurants & Institutions,
Delta Air Lines' *Sky, Business Atlanta* (the October 1987
edition put me into the Atlanta 100 Private Companies
as Entrepreneur of the Year), *Georgia Trend,* the *Atlanta
Journal & Constitution,* and other restaurant and trade
publications and nationwide newspapers too numer-
ous to mention.

In February 1986, *Business Atlanta* featured our
company and its leadership in the cover story, "King of
the Malls," calling Chick-fil-A "one of Atlanta's most
visible home-grown companies."

Chick-fil-A was the top-rated chicken chain restaurant in the eighth annual "America's Choice in Chains
Consumer Satisfaction Survey" sponsored by *Restaurants & Institutions* magazine and reported in its February 5, 1988, issue.

The "Choice in Chains" survey is conducted for the
magazine by the National Family Opinion research
firm with a 1,400 mail sampling from its consumer
panel of 375,000 households, the largest consumer
panel in America. The NFO panel rated chain restaurants they have actually visited on the basis of satisfaction.

Our own consumer research, conducted semiannu-
ally by Marketing and Research Counselors, Inc.,
shows consumers have ranked Chick-fil-A highest for
overall food quality and taste for six consecutive years.
In the research, consumers show their preference for
Chick-fil-A menu items time and time again by rating
the chicken sandwich and Nuggets® number one in
taste and quality over all major fast-food competitors.

Chick-fil-A could have gone in many directions at
the beginning. We could have sold franchises or stock,

or I could have borrowed the money myself, then sought qualified individuals who had the time, commitment, and dedication to undertake their assignments.

Stanley Marcus, retired chairman of Neiman-Marcus, said, "A public corporation concentrates on profits while a private company concentrates on its people." By operating one of the country's largest privately held restaurant chains, Chick-fil-A has been able to do a lot of things that would not be allowed by others in the industry. For example, as a public company, we could not easily give away brand-new Lincoln automobiles, sponsor annual business seminars in posh resorts, offer $1,000 scholarships to our young people, or help to support WinShape Centre at Berry College, to name a few projects.

The advance of the company has not always been smooth and without testings. First came the pioneering Unit at the Greenbriar Mall in Atlanta, then one at Savannah and one at Burlington, North Carolina. That third restaurant was an eye-opener. Our Operator struggled to show a profit, but there were still not sufficient sales. We transferred him to Columbia, South Carolina, where he became highly successful, and we put the third Unit under the managing directorship of a dedicated employee. Later the restaurant began to prosper.

In 1971, we had our first annual seminar at which all seven Operators gathered. We were planning to open fourteen new Units in 1974 at the height of the terrible inflation surge. Units were costing $75,000, but inflation tacked on another $25,000 so that they ran $100,000 each—a total of $350,000 over what had been budgeted to build them.

I had to sign away everything but my wife to borrow $600,000 and continue expanding. When you borrow that much money, few banks will even talk to you about it. In 1975, Chick-fil-A enjoyed a sales increase of 76 percent, and that put us back on a sound financial base. But worse struggles for the business lay ahead.

Chick-fil-A made a noticeable decline in 1982. I couldn't figure out why. We had the best-trained personnel. We worked hard. We had a fine product. Then I realized what had happened. Other fast-food chains had awakened to what Chick-fil-A had been doing. They, too, had entered the chicken sandwich business. For a period of time, they managed to cut into our sales.

As a businessman, I knew only one way to combat the competition, and that involved putting on a strong promotional campaign. We started the breast-of-chicken idea, and we believed then, as I believe today, that we have the best chicken product available. We notified Operators of our campaign and put coupons in papers all over the country; we alloted 3.25 percent of our total sales for the redemption of the coupons.

Then came another problem. Our campaign was so successful that the coupon redemption cost ran to nearly 7 percent of sales. We were glad for the success, but while it showed that people were eating Chick-fil-A, it also hit us hard in the pocketbook. I didn't want the Operators to have to pay for the unexpected rise in advertising costs, even though they benefited in the long run.

"Chick-fil-A Incorporated will absorb the difference," I told my executive staff and the Operators. The staff agreed with my decision, but I saw a few worried faces. It put a heavier strain on an already strained cash flow.

On the morning of April 1, I sat in my office on the

fifth floor of our new office building. Two floors were still not completed, but they would be finished soon. I looked outside. The trees had filled their branches with green leaves, and the air had turned warm. Below, two young men were planting jonquils alongside the path between the building and the parking lots. It was a quiet, peaceful atmosphere.

I should have been happy and on top of the world, but I was concerned about the cash-flow problem and the squeeze of finances. Because I've always been wary of heavy debt, I just didn't know how to avoid worrying about it. I didn't have much choice but to keep on going. But I thought a lot about the situation and talked it over often with Jeannette and Jimmy Collins. We came to one conclusion: God was still directing us, and somehow it would all work out.

Many are the times that I have thanked God for Jimmy Collins. He joined Chick-fil-A in 1968, leaving the food service design consulting company he had owned for five years. He had faith in our concepts and felt a divine call to Chick-fil-A. We make a good team. He is committed to excellence and is knowledgeable about how to make a company grow.

Jimmy had assisted in the design of the Forest Park Dwarf House and had helped to lay out the equipment. It was a significant day in the late sixties when Jimmy came on board.

At the 1988 seminar, I named Jimmy the president of Chick-fil-A, and I claimed the position of chairman of the board, continuing to serve as its chief executive officer. This was a complete surprise to Jimmy who had served for twenty years as executive vice president. I was happy that my son Dan had urged me to make the appointment. Jimmy has a great breadth of understanding in the corporation's marketing, accounting, and legal operations, and he reads a hundred books a year. He also offers perceptive analysis concerning each new applicant. He is committed both to the company and to the people in it.

Commitment characterizes all of my associates. I like what my son Dan, senior vice president of operations, told a reporter for *Business Atlanta,* "The pure and simple bottom line at Chick-fil-A is a commitment to people, and that's the staff, Operators, crew, and the public. From the outset we wanted to have a positive influence on all who came in contact with Chick-fil-A." My younger son, Bubba, vice president of development, added, "The restaurants are simply the vehicles by which we serve that purpose."

Even though our company had enjoyed the blessing of God, that didn't make us immune to problems. The recession of 1982 was a clear example of that. I didn't take a salary that year because I didn't want our employees to take pay cuts. I struggled with this, but I also was determined not to lose sleep over it.

More than once, interested companies approached me about selling out. In the early stages of Chick-fil-A, Morrison's Cafeterias offered me an attractive figure if I would remain as head of the company for five years. I was pleased with the offer, and it was somewhat tempting at the time. But money was not my goal in life, and I didn't want to work for somebody else. I thought of more recent offers to buy us out. The dollar figures got larger, but I still didn't want to sell. And I couldn't sell when we were in trouble. That would be like running away. Chick-fil-A from the beginning has been a family-type enterprise, so I couldn't just selfishly quit.

Regardless of the severity of the situation, in most

instances I have been able to dismiss the problems from my mind and get a good night's sleep. A fellow restaurateur advised me, "If you can get a good night's rest, you can cope with any problem; since you can't solve problems with your head on your pillow, why even try?"

Finally, in October of 1982, I hit bottom. I kept asking, "God, where have I failed You?" I knew I was not responsible for everything that happens, but I can't seem to operate differently. If business goes down, I take that as my responsibility. I kept praying that the Lord would help me and, if I had personally failed Him, that I would correct it. I finally shared all of this with my family and then with my executive staff.

Most of them had known things weren't going well, but they didn't know how bad it was or how deeply troubled I was. I felt my own loss of worth, and I hadn't been able to rise above it.

I couldn't ignore the dismal sales figures. The first real sales decrease in our company's history occurred in 1982. Our actual sales had fallen off, even though we had more restaurants.

I looked at the problems facing us. Five malls had been scheduled to open but were delayed by the developers for months. We had geared our whole program toward the malls' target dates. That meant we had to pay Operators who had no restaurants. We couldn't advertise or do anything until the malls opened.

Four restaurants were delayed for nearly two years. We had to shift personnel around because of that. In each case the mall developers had encountered serious problems that forced them to delay their projected openings.

Other malls opened, but instead of nearly all the space being filled, which usually happens with a well-planned shopping center venture, in several cases fewer than half the spaces had been occupied. And we learned quickly that having the mall filled with stores brings customers to us.

On top of that, the American economy went crazy with incredible inflation. Interest rates shot up as high as 23 percent, which is what we had to pay for a period of time.

I felt squeezed. I was afraid of debt, yet I had signed a lease on some properties and couldn't walk away from them. No matter what I looked at or where I turned, the situation got worse. I couldn't understand what was happening.

In October I called our executive staff to a special meeting away from our facilities so that we could think more objectively. We chose Pine Isle Hotel on Lake Lanier, an hour's drive north of the city, as our retreat. We looked at figures, graphs, and projections. We gave explanations, reasons, and even excuses, but none of it solved anything.

During the long discussion, as we sat around a circular table, my older son Dan spoke up. (Dan is the real administrator in the family and far more systematic in his approach than the rest of us.) "Why are we in business?" he asked. "Why are we here? Why are we alive?"

At first I considered these to be simple questions. Why are we wasting time talking about the *why* when we need to talk about more important things, such as *how* are we going to get past this crisis? Instead of brushing his questions aside, however, I stopped. "Maybe we do need to answer those questions," I said.

We looked at one another in silence. Some glanced at the ceiling or walls of that quiet room at the Pine Isle Hotel. We had no schedule to keep, no pressing business appointments, and no phone calls waiting. We had purposely chosen an isolated spot. As I've learned so often in life, people need to get away from a problem in order to solve it. Sitting in the midst of the trouble only makes people more conscious of the negative forces.

"I can think of five or six reasons," someone finally said, and the discussion began.

Each of us honestly tried to verbalize why we were in the business. Since all of us on the executive staff are church members and have declared our faith in Jesus Christ, it did not take long before we started talking about the religious aspects. I'm a Christian ready to talk to anyone about the influence of Jesus Christ in my life, but I've hesitated to make public statements about my faith or about the company in such a way, trying to capitalize on the fact that most of our people are Christians. I don't like the idea of parading my religious faith. I want it to show by my lifestyle and by the way I treat people.

As we continued to share our thoughts, we came to a unanimous agreement. We all decided that our purpose in being in business needed to reflect the belief that God plays a major role in our lives. We also decided that we wanted to make a statement for our own benefit, one that reflected our true beliefs. We had no intention of posting it as a statement of faith or using it as a prerequisite for becoming part of Chick-fil-A.

"I think we need to remind ourselves that we are stewards . . . caretakers . . . servants of what God gives us," Bubba said.

We finally wrote down two statements:

CORPORATE PURPOSE

1. To glorify God by being a faithful steward of all that is entrusted to us.
2. To have a positive influence on all who come in contact with Chick-fil-A.

These two statements sound simple enough, but none of us were theologians. We worked on them a good part of a morning, adding words and taking away others. Everyone present absorbed himself in the discussion until we all felt satisfied. We weren't trying to be exact in what we wrote down, but we wanted our corporate statement to state truly our convictions.

"Our customers might never know our 'Corporate Purpose,'" noted Steve Robinson, vice president of marketing, "but we know. And God knows."

That statement summarizes my attitude better than anything else. I have always wanted to influence the people in our organization, not by pressing anything on them, but by my attitude, my lifestyle.

"We know our stance," said Buck McCabe, vice president of finance. "But now what?"

"How do we make these concepts known to our Operators?" asked Bureon Ledbetter, vice president and general counsel.

"We can't stop with just having a few statements printed nicely for our offices," Dan added. "We have to have a way to make certain our Operators know where Chick-fil-A stands."

"Print it up for every Operator as part of our training program," Jimmy Collins suggested.

Eventually, we came up with a unique idea. We would design a desk accessory to hold paper clips and pens. On a small plaque we would print our two state-

158   IT'S EASIER TO SUCCEED

ments and make certain that every Operator and staff person had one. In a subtle way we wanted to say what we stood for.

That was only the first important item for us to discuss that day. We still had to talk about our spring promotional campaign and our decreasing sales.

We sat around analyzing *why*. It didn't take long to admit our shortsightedness. We had been moving along steadily for a few years with no serious drawbacks, but we had not figured on such things as the slumping economy, the increased competition, some Operators not doing a good job, and so on. We had to motivate our home office staff and our Operators. We wanted to be faithful to our statements, but we were also in business to make a profit. I knew the two could work together.

Our sales, just over $100 million annually in 1982, had attracted the competition's attention. Actually, the competition posed less of a threat than we had feared. We were the first to use chicken breast fillets, and all of them were trying to follow our example. But we didn't think that they were doing it as well or that their products were anywhere near equal to ours.

I remember saying, "There's always a market for the best. Most people know we were the first." That led to the promotional slogan "First 'n' Best."

At that meeting, we all emphasized the importance of QSC—Quality, Service, Cleanliness. "No matter what our campaigns and our promos are, let's keep QSC first," Bubba said.

We came away from that retreat more determined than ever to stress those three words to our Operators by mail, by phone, and by personal visits to their restaurants. By the time the heavy Christmas season was upon us, our promotion had paid off. We saw an increase in our sales volume. By April 1983, just six months later, our sales had increased 40.35 percent over 1982.

We can find reasons why this happened: our moving aggressively, our taking charge of the situation, and our fighting the competition. At the same time, I also believe that God honored our commitment. It was the first time that the executive staff had ever formed any kind of statement. Yet, each of us felt it represented not only a statement but also a positive commitment from us as individuals. We would also use it as our incentive as we moved ahead.

As a Christmas gift in 1983, the staff gave me a huge bronze plaque measuring two feet by three feet on which was engraved our corporate purpose. Below the inscription, they had written: "S. Truett Cathy, Founder."

As we discussed the proper place to mount this beautiful gift, Cos Walker, senior director of our northeast region, suggested mounting it outside the front door where it would call to our attention each day why we are coming to work. We had a base built to blend in with the exterior of the corporate headquarters building, and we placed it outside the front entrance.

This gesture meant a lot to me at the time, especially since the staff people had given it to me. The years have made it even more meaningful.

Is it unusual for a business to establish such a statement as its purpose? I don't think so. All supernatural resources come from God. Just as an individual receives power, strength, and wisdom from God, so a corporation, which is a collective body of people, can enjoy power, strength, and wisdom for every undertaking.

Within a year from the time we drafted our purpose,

the company changed direction. That was when I studied the 1983 figures and marveled at the sales increase of 29 percent nationwide. That year we awarded forty-six Mark VII Lincoln Continentals to Operators whose business had jumped ahead by at least 40 percent.

Maybe that's how life works for many of us. We face a crisis and do everything we can, but we also call on God for help. Then we often don't recognize it as God's doing when it actually happens. Often we see God working only much later when we reflect on the event. And if we're not careful, we accept it all as something *we* have done. We forget about God's gracious involvement.

I might have done that, too, except for the timing of events. We made our public commitment to our Operators at a low financial point. That statement could have brought us ridicule and bad responses from our people, but we had to take our stand. And then, everything else began to fit together.

We haven't denied our commitment to our values and beliefs, but we haven't tried to publicize them. I don't want people coming to Chick-fil-A just because we sometimes talk about God. I want them to come because of the quality of our people, our product, our service, and the inviting atmosphere.

"What comes first in your life, Truett?" someone asked me at a businessmen's luncheon.

That's a hard question for me to answer. And maybe it depends on what you mean by "first." I am in business, and I give my work all that I can. God is important, and so is my family. I remain as active in church as I can, but sometimes business activities take me away from church. Rather than talk about first or second or third place, I try to blend together my attitudes toward God, toward my family, and toward my business.

One of my values is that I honor God by being a successful businessman. As a Christian, I think I can glorify God best by success and not by failure.

Not everybody sees it that way. "You ought to be in church and never miss" is the way some look at it. Maybe they're right.

One time recently we arranged for people to film the Chick-fil-A headquarters and then take pictures of my family and me, both at the office and at home. We had expected to have it all finished by midday. I had to cancel two appointments that afternoon. I had planned to attend a church committee meeting at 7:30. But by 6:00, it became obvious that the camera crew would be with us for at least two more hours. I had to cancel my church engagement. In that case, some might say that I put my business first. I can only answer that I did what I thought best.

In recent years I've been receiving more and more invitations to speak to business meetings, civic groups, churches, schools, clubs, and luncheons. I'm smart enough to know that they ask me because I've become successful in business, not because I'm such a great speaker. If I still had one restaurant in Hapeville, I don't think I'd have the same number of invitations.

We constantly change our promotions and campaigns and even our emphasis. We're now moving into free-standing restaurants in addition to the mall restaurants. But the basic principles of business and of life never change. Of one thing we are certain: God will continue to bring into our lives many surprises to increase our faith. If we walk hand in hand with Him, it is easier to succeed than to fail.

11

THE $10 MILLION TREE HOUSE

From the tiny office a block from the Dwarf House where Brooksie Kirk first went to work in 1964 to the present center of operations a quarter of a century later, Chick-fil-A has come a long way. In 1984, the *Atlanta Business Chronicle* cited our facilities as being one of the six most beautiful corporate headquarters in Metro Atlanta. That put us, a privately held organization, in the company of AT&T, Georgia-Pacific, Coca-Cola, and other huge national giants.

Our five-story office building in an idyllic spot among dogwood and oak trees on seventy-five acres of forested land is the culmination of nearly three decades of growth. As our business expanded, we kept running out of office space. In 1967, I bought an air-freight building on Virginia Avenue, near the Atlanta airport. It met our immediate needs, so I didn't think much about future office expansion. The building provided some office space, but we used most of it as a warehouse. Gradually the expanding office operations made the warehouse space smaller and smaller, though.

We bought an empty mobile home and parked it alongside. Then we purchased two houses next door to the air-freight building. At the Tri-City Federal Building, located a mile away, we rented one and a half floors. For a few months, those measures took care of the problem. None of us had any idea how fast our organization would grow. Even if we had, we couldn't have afforded to start with a large place. I kept looking for property to buy; every time I spotted a large, empty building, I investigated. But nothing seemed quite what I wanted.

One opportunity looked exciting. Not far from the airport, a commercial area developed around Phoenix Center. We liked the area, but while we were negotiating for fifteen acres, the Shell Oil Company bought the entire plot.

The matter of finding a suitable building became an ever-increasing problem. If the location and price looked right, the property would not allow for expansion. I didn't want to move again in three to five years. I made up my mind that I wanted a corporation headquarters where we could house our executive offices, provide a place for training our Operators, and have sufficient warehouse space, all under one roof. No such place seemed to exist.

Many times I thought of buying land and building what we needed, but that didn't seem to work out either. When I found suitable land, the price range exceeded the amount I felt we could afford. I kept searching, and I prayed often about it.

One day I was sitting in my office, chatting with an old friend in the real estate business. Casually he said, "By the way, Truett, I know where you could possibly get a good deal on seventy-five acres of land."

"A hundred miles from Atlanta?" I asked when he told me the price.

✳ ──────────────────────────

*Doing things right
the first time
every time
is the
Chick-fil-A
Quality Policy
program*

──────────────────────────

He shook his head. "I just heard about it. The land is just south of I-285, only four miles from the new airport terminal.

"The land," he went on, "has been in foreclosure for seven years by Wells Fargo of Houston, Texas."

I decided to look at it. I had investigated so many places in the past three years that I had almost lost hope of finding anything suitable. But when I drove out and saw the property, I felt good about it. With frontage on the Atlanta interstate loop, it seemed right for me.

I immediately thought of all we could do to develop that land so that it could be practical and beautiful while preserving as much of the natural environment as possible. I had always wanted a building nestled among trees. What is the use of selecting a beautiful piece of wooded property, erecting a building, and then asphalting everything for parking?

After our offer for the property was accepted, we designed a modern building with the aid of an architect and staff people. I wanted our headquarters to be the kind of place I could be proud of, a place of comfortable, efficient design that would delight both employee and visitor.

We engaged Phil Smallwood with the company of Smallwood, Reynolds, Stewart and Stewart and Associates to design the building. As we walked together among the dogwood and oak, I shared my goals with the architect. Our building should serve people with all the light and color and woodland we could keep.

Early sketches showed a huge skylight at the top and an atrium in the center five floors high around which the offices were arranged. Line by line, the design of the building took shape like a work of art. By the summer of 1981, construction was in full swing.

I'll never forget that April morning when I drove down our entrance road three-quarters of a mile long, past our own small lake where ducks were swimming, past trees budding in the new springtime, past the early flowers and new-mown grass to the beautiful building with an abundance of windows that had become the office of our company and the workaday world of our employees. No matter how many times I go into our headquarters, I still like to pause, stare up at it, and silently thank God for helping to make it happen.

We spent close to $10 million on the glass-and-concrete headquarters with its beautiful furnishings. It has an eighty-foot atrium lobby, a five-story spiral staircase at one end, and glass-enclosed elevators on the other. We tried to provide the latest in design and equipment. I even have a Jacuzzi in my executive suite, which has become a place people want to see when they tour our headquarters.

A food service staff provides a delicious cafeteria-style lunch for employees and visitors. We also have a fitness center in the basement. Bright colors, an open design, and good lighting in our building help the employees to feel proud of their office home.

At our open house we routinely put ashtrays everywhere. It was kind of an invitation for visitors and employees to smoke, although very few of the staff did so. We realized one day that only three members of our staff used tobacco. Two of them left, so that meant that only one employee smoked cigarettes. That person took it upon himself to quit, leaving our office free of smoke.

We gathered up the ashtrays and took them away. A sign at the reception desk reads: "Smoking is permitted outside." Out there we find that the Lord cleans up the air quite nicely. Sales people visiting the offices sometimes look around to see if anyone is smoking. If they don't see anyone else using cigarettes, they usually don't light up, and that suits us just fine.

As a gift to me one Christmas, my staff from each of our twenty-one departments had Scripture verses engraved in wood and mounted on trees along our nature walk. Visitors, including many children, take that walk and read the verses.

Within our large lobby we have space for special programs at Christmas and other seasons.

Our building, with 110,000 square feet adequate for up to 325 employees, has heavily indebted us, but I am not greatly concerned. We qualified for industrial revenue bonds, and that got us a very reasonable interest rate.

The right kind of operating base makes it easier to recruit the kind of people we want to be associated with, offers room for expansion without moving, and makes it easier for our staff to succeed in their respective departments.

Oftentimes visitors will remark, "Truett, I would work here for free." I tell our staff people they have to work extremely hard to stay on the payroll because people offer their services "for free." I haven't tested these people for their sincerity, however.

12

WINSHAPE

*S*ix *months after we moved into our new* headquarters building another bold, new service opportunity presented itself. For me, it was a real desire fulfilled, an extension of my work with young people, and an opportunity upon which to build for the future.

It all began when I accepted an invitation to speak at Berry College at Mount Berry on the outskirts of Rome, Georgia, a two-hour drive northwest of Atlanta. The college had been founded by Martha Berry approximately eighty years earlier. She wanted not only to provide the best in education and to challenge the minds of the young, but also to help students develop spiritual aspects of life. Classes and curricula reflect those emphases today. Berry College also has a physical work program. By stressing the need to develop the hands, the college helps young people learn skills, good work habits, and healthy attitudes toward life.

The administrators of the college asked me to serve as visiting professor in their business school on November 28 and 29, 1982. When I arrived on campus, Dean Ouida Dickey set up an extended tour. I've been to a lot of places over the years, but that school had something different about it. The sheer beauty of the grounds and the entire area of twenty-eight thousand acres delighted me. The caliber of the students impressed me as well. They seemed to be some of the most dedicated I had ever seen. I was amazed to see female students driving tractors. At Berry, the students are given cooperative responsibility for the grounds; they have a sense that it is "their" campus.

After I left the college, I couldn't get it out of my thoughts, and so I spread the news of my impressions everywhere I went. A few months later when I had the responsibility for the program at the Rotary Club of the Atlanta airport area, I phoned Dr. Gloria Shatto, president of Berry College, and asked her to be our speaker.

On July 18, 1983, Dr. Shatto came to our luncheon to talk about the ideals and programs of Berry College. She described the place as "Georgia's best-kept secret."

As we chatted during lunch, Dr. Shatto mentioned a sad situation facing the administration at Berry. "We've had to make a most agonizing decision," she said. "We've closed our academy. We are talking with people from a number of organizations who are interested in using the facilities. The campus is not for sale, but we are looking for someone who will use the facilities in a manner compatible with Berry College and its mission." (The academy, located on the Mountain Campus three miles from the main campus had programs for grades five through twelve.)

The sadness on her face and in her voice revealed how strongly the decision had affected her. When she mentioned grades five through twelve, she really got my attention. I remembered the boys of those ages that Jeannette and I had tried to help down through the years. I also thought of the efforts of Martha Berry and

*———————————————

*We never realize
our greatest potential
until we perform
at our very best.*

———————————————

others who helped support the school in its infancy. Henry Ford, Andrew Carnegie, and Teddy Roosevelt were some who had devoted their finances and efforts toward helping worthy young people. Now some young people would not have a place to attend school.

Rising costs and low student enrollment were among the main reasons for closing the school, Dr. Shatto said. Martha Berry had established a school for poor rural youth. Over the past few decades, the student body had changed, and Berry Academy had become a school out of tune with the mission of the early school and of the contemporary college. In addition, good public schools in the area could now meet the original need addressed by Martha Berry.

"It's a shame to close that beautiful place," I remarked.

Dr. Shatto turned to me with her dark eyes focused on my face and asked a simple question. I know she was merely making conversation and did not expect an answer from me when she asked, "Have you any ideas?"

"Well, no," I said truthfully, wishing I had had a dozen of them. "It will take someone with a lot of vision to utilize that facility."

"That it will," she replied.

Our conversation moved on to other things. After Dr. Shatto spoke to our club, I drove her to the airport and she left on a fund-raising trip for Berry.

I thought about that school for days. I kept hearing Dr. Shatto's soft voice asking, "Have you any ideas?" Finally, I decided to visit Berry College again.

"Would you like to go with me?" I asked Jeannette. "It's less than a two-hour ride."

"Why do you want to go there?"

"I don't know," I said, "but I can't get that place out of my mind."

Jeannette shares my vision about young people. I thought of the children's homes that I have contact with and of all those deserving young people who need a chance in life. At the same time, Berry College had all those facilities going unused. Somehow there had to be a way to tie all that together.

"I'm just curious," I told my wife.

I said the same thing to John Lipscomb when he met us. He escorted us around the entire campus. Again the beauty captivated me. Frost Chapel overwhelmed us with its quiet sense of reverence. In the woodworking shop my mind could see young people learning how to use their hands as they improved their minds and hearts. Everywhere we went I saw the same simple beauty from the library to the dormitories to the lighted tennis court and the well-kept track.

I shook my head. "All of this standing idle. . . ."

As Jeannette and I rode and walked across the spacious campus, I thought of the times I had responded when churches and groups had asked for help to build camping facilities for their people. Yet here at Berry were facilities with no one using them. I sensed that I had to become involved in the answer to Dr. Shatto's question. "But how?"

I thought of the more than fifteen thousand young people who work for Chick-fil-A on a part-time basis. I thought of our incentive program that offers them a scholarship of $1,000 toward tuition at a college of their choice. One of my great joys has been to award over five thousand of those scholarships since 1973. We have offered this scholarship with no obligation to

Chick-fil-A. I like to think this is planting good seeds that will bear future fruit.

Why not connect our scholarship program with the vision and goals of Berry College? That way, the money could provide an opportunity to young people and also stimulate the folks at Berry College to get involved.

Then I had an idea: *Why not establish the academy as our own campus!* The implications of that idea started to take shape. Scholarship recipients could live in the dormitories and study at the main campus of Berry College three miles down the road. Those buildings would serve people the way Miss Berry had intended.

Tears clouded my eyes as I considered how many lives we could help shape through programs at Berry. What an opportunity! I could help young people and do it with the cooperation of Berry's facilities.

"What do you think of this place?" I asked Jeannette before mentioning a word about the thoughts going through my mind.

"I feel as if I'm standing on holy ground," she said.

I don't often feel that God Himself is leading me into something, but I did that day. I knew without doubt that I had a role to play in fulfilling the vision of Martha Berry. Before we left, I told John Lipscomb what I had in mind. I wanted to see what he thought about it. His beaming face would have told me his response even if he had not said a word. He expressed immediate interest in the proposal. He made some suggestions, asked questions, and helped me to clarify my ideas.

We returned to Dr. Shatto's office. I said, "You asked me one day if I had any ideas on how to use the Mountain Campus. Well, I didn't then, but I do now."

Then we discussed our concept with Dr. Shatto. "Sounds terrific!" she said. We talked a long time and even prayed together.

In that one day, the full concept evolved for using the Mountain Campus in helping able young people (including many who worked for Chick-fil-A) attend Berry College. Our broad plan included the possibility of a summer camp for young people and a foster home for children with that need. By the time we parted, we had agreed tentatively on an outline of plans that emerged without significant change as WinShape Centre.

We had a thousand details to work out. The Board of Trustees at Berry had to approve my proposal—and they did with enthusiasm. I wanted them to know that I didn't make the offer to get students to work for Chick-fil-A then or later. I told the trustees, "I have a concern to help deserving young people. I want them to make the best of their time, and I want to help them develop their talents to be their very best."

As the program took shape during the next few months, Dr. Shatto remarked one day, "Truett, do you realize that this is, to my knowledge, the first time that private business and education have cooperated in a joint venture of this kind to reach specific goals?" She pointed out that conglomerates often endow schools and sometimes build buildings, but as far as she knew, no company had done anything like what we were proposing. We were entering into a unique agreement.

"This is very exciting," she said, "and I'm eager to see how it will all work out."

As we talked, wrote, phoned, and discussed and rediscussed every issue over the next several months, the vision began to take shape. Scholarships would be offered to worthy young people who have demonstrated

leadership and who meet the entrance requirements of
Berry College.

We first set up a nonprofit foundation; Chick-fil-A
would be the primary sponsor. For the 1984–85 school
year, the goal was for 50 to 75 students. We enrolled 68.
The present facilities will accommodate approximately
125 students, but it was decided it would be good to
start with a smaller number. We established a name for
the facility as WinShape Centre—"Shaping individuals
to be winners."

For the 1984–85 school term, we offered $4,000—
half paid by Chick-fil-A and half by Berry College. This
amount represents full tuition for the first school year.
The scholarship is reduced to $3,000 for the second
year, $2,000 for the third, and $1,000 for the fourth
year.

Students live on the academy's campus, which has
total boarding facilities. They can earn between $900
and $1,800 through an on-campus work program of at
least ten hours a week. Berry College doesn't require
students to work, but well over 90 percent of them par-
ticipate in some form of work programs, choosing their
area of interest from 110 departments. One student describes Berry as a "multitude of student workers and a
handful of supervisors, which makes us know it's our
college."

This scholarship arrangement helps young people
without doing everything for them. They need the most
help to get started in college. Once started, they can
usually find a way to keep going.

Out of the reviving of the academy's campus grew
Camp WinShape for Boys in 1985, a summer program
for boys eight through sixteen on the campus. By 1988,
the program enrolled 472 boys. I suggested the theme:

"It is better to build boys than to mend men." The program seeks to develop the whole person, challenging each boy to do his best at all he does.

Operated through our WinShape Foundation, the camp involves boys in Indian lore programs. Opportunities to learn about Indian costumes, authentic Indian dances, mannerisms, and heritage are afforded to each camper. The kids earn different Indian ranks as they develop morally, physically, and spiritually at Camp WinShape each summer. Four tennis courts, a swimming pool, gymnasium, archery range, riflery range, fifteen-acre lake, dining hall, two dormitories, and dozens of trails to explore—the kids have it all. I often say to the boys, "You have a twenty-eight-thousand-acre playground."

In the summer of 1987, a girls' camp was initiated at WinShape with housing at the Ford Buildings on the main campus of Berry College. That year, 116 girls participated in the camp, which emphasized horseback skills. Eighteen horses were used for the program, now being expanded. By 1988, the number of girls doubled to 232, and more are projected for the coming years. The age range for girls is also eight through sixteen.

A foster home has been established, and a new five-thousand-square-foot home has been built for full-time parents and up to seventeen children. It will cater to kids who have no behavioral problems—good students, and those striving for achievements regardless of the circumstances. Many young people rise above their circumstances simply because they're determined to be winners.

I'm proud of the leadership that we have been able to attract to administer the WinShape program. Every child they build will be one less adult to mend.

The following remarks are excerpts from Truett Cathy's address to the Berry College student body on Founder's Day, 1984:

According to records at the Jefferson Davis Research Center, back in 1800, one hundred years before Martha Berry established the Berry Schools, the Bible was the major textbook in American schools. Approximately 90 percent of the curriculum dealt with the development of the student's character. By 1921, this had deteriorated to only 6 percent. And in our present day, it is so insignificant that it is hardly measurable.

When I went to school in the late 1920s, on a normal day in our classroom we would open with a Scripture reading. After that, we would repeat the Lord's Prayer in unison and pledge allegiance to the American flag before sitting down to study.

I wonder today how many schools open with Scripture reading and prayer, followed by the pledge of allegiance. I wonder if we haven't lost some of the important things that enable people to learn what they need to know. As Vice President John Lipscomb brought out in his message, the important things never change. We are in a changing world, but as you think back, the important things do not change.

Martha Berry was aware of a need. She had her priorities in the proper order: first the establishment of a Sunday school where the Bible was taught and Scripture verses memorized, and then training in elementary education.

Martha Berry had a God-given insight into the need and the importance of developing the spiritual aspect of a person's life. We read in the Scripture that we are created in the image and likeness of God for the purpose of serving and glorifying God.

Martha Berry was aware of the need to develop a person's mind, to stimulate him or her to find the great resources of the mind, and to have the ability to gain wisdom that he or she might make good decisions that will yield good results. She had faith in the lowly, believing that a person could accomplish anything, regardless of the circumstances, if offered an opportunity and a challenge to reach certain goals.

A man who carried newspapers as a boy determined in his mind that someday he would become the editor of that newspaper, and so he did. While addressing a group of people many years later, he said, "My one disappointment in myself is that I did not set my goals high enough. I could just as surely have become editor of the *New York Times*, had I set my goals high enough."

Sometimes we fail to achieve certain goals simply because we do not set our goals high enough. Usually a person can accomplish the things that he sets his mind to accomplish.

This philosophy is completely compatible with Chick-fil-A. Our corporate purpose is this: "To glorify God by being a faithful steward of all that is entrusted to us, and to have a positive influence on all who come in contact with Chick-fil-A."

I am motivated by the performance of our young people. We employ in our various restaurants more than twelve thousand young people. We find that many work simply because they like to work. Others work because they are compelled to do so by the necessities of life.

An Operator in Texas told about two young ladies who worked in his restaurant. He said they would drive up in a brand-new automobile about every six months. They lived in such an affluent home that they had a twenty-four-hour guard on duty. Naturally, these girls did not have to work, but they did so because they enjoyed working.

In Cincinnati, Ohio, the operator of our restaurant there told me often about an amazing fellow named Bert, so it was my great pleasure to have him visit in our home.

Bert had graduated from high school at the age of sixteen with a grade point average of 4.2. He was the principal breadwinner for his family because his daddy walked off when Bert was thirteen. His mother was unable to work, and he had a ten-year-old sister.

I asked Bert how much he earned in a year. He said, "About $3,000."

"How much of that were you able to keep for yourself?" I asked.

"About $50," he replied.

I pressed him further. "I don't mean just spending money. I'm talking about money for clothes and school expenses and all that."

"Well, just about $50," he repeated. "Everything else went to Mom for the family."

Since the age of five, Bert has wanted to be a medical doctor. No one told him how expensive medical school was going to be. He has graduated from Ohio State, and has been accepted at Mercer University in Macon, Georgia. He has high moral standards and a glowing personality—the kind of individual you just love to have around.

We at Chick-fil-A feel that being in the food business gives us the opportunity to provide a necessity of life—food. We want to play an important part in the emotional and physical needs of the people we serve, and often in their spiritual needs as well.

As you already know, Chick-fil-A and Berry College have entered into a unique arrangement to foster the moral, educational, and spiritual development of young people. President Gloria Shatto, Vice President John Lipscomb, faculty, trustees, students, and all those who have invested their time and resources in this place, and to the legacy of Martha Berry, I pledge to you my influence and my cooperative spirit to uphold the requests of Martha Berry in her last written letter addressed to the graduates in which she said,

> Use all your influence to hold the school to the original plan of simple living, work, prayer, the Bible being taught, Christian teachers keeping the schools a separate community, protecting and guarding the property in the good name of the school. My prayer is that the schools may stand through the ages for the honor and glory of God.

Most of you know that those words were attached to Miss Berry's will and were opened after her death. We all have an obligation to fulfill the desire of the founder, and I am committed today to be a part of this effort.

In closing, I wish to quote a Chinese proverb that says, "If we plant for days, we plant flowers; if we plant for years, we plant trees, but if we plant for eternity, we plant ideas and ideals into the lives of others."

Thank you.

FAMILIAR QUOTATIONS BY MARTHA BERRY

PERSONAL MOTTO: "Prayer Changes Things."

"I pray that I may leave the world more beautiful than I found it."

"We walk into tomorrow on the lives of our youth."

"The best way to help anyone is to give him a chance to help himself."

"Beauty is a part of education."

"I have walked too far on my plank of faith to turn back."

"God has been as good to me as I would let Him be."

"God is the real founder of Berry College. I am only the human founder."

"There is so much to do and so little time."

"Education combines the head, hand, and heart."

"Young people should lift their eyes to spires, to hill-tops, and to God."

"Our country needs people who work for a Higher Master and higher pay than salary checks."

"When I can no longer work for Berry, the Alumni and friends will continue the work."

"Not to be ministered unto, but to minister."

"I've put everything I have into boys and girls, the soundest investment there is, and no slump can wipe out the returns."

"People are more important than ideas."

13

IMPORTANT THINGS DO NOT CHANGE

Although it is easier to succeed than to fail, I do not mean to imply with the title of this book that it's *easy* to succeed. Success has a temporary price that we pay for future dividends. Always keep in mind the priorities of life—why we are alive, why God created us, and for what purpose we are alive.

In a sermon on the priorities of life, my pastor related a news article written by an irresponsible reporter. The story told of a small-town merchant who was robbed and murdered on his way home from work on a Saturday evening. The news account gave details of the incident and closed with this line: "Fortunately for the deceased, he had dropped his money in the night depository before he was murdered, and the only thing that was lost was his life."

Would you be willing to sacrifice your life for all of your material possessions? "For what profit is it to a man," the Bible asks, "if he gains the whole world and loses his own soul?"

What is important to you? What are your priorities? What is most meaningful and precious to you that cannot be purchased with dollars?

A father was pushing his infant son in a stroller

along the sidewalk of his community when a neighbor joined him. "How much would you take for your son?" the neighbor asked.

"You know the answer to that," his friend replied. "I wouldn't take $1 million for him."

One of the men moved his family to a distant city shortly after that. Sixteen years later, the neighbors had a reunion. "How is that precious little boy?" said one.

"You wouldn't believe it," answered the other man. "He's been in all types of trouble . . . has caused our family lots of heartache. Why, he's not worth a dime."

What happens to cause such a devaluation of a human being? How do people go wrong?

When I speak to fathers, and often to fathers and sons together, I try to point out that the father is the chairman of the board, the president, and the CEO of the greatest institution in the world—the home. Home is the main teaching station; parents are the principal teachers. School is not the main teaching station; church is not the main teaching station; it is the home. Children are crying out, pleading from their hearts, "Come on, Mom and Dad, show us God's success formula through your example."

Scripture teaches that God should be first, others second, and self last. The Scripture also teaches us to fear and reverence God as we use common sense.

A pastor friend felt the need to resign from his pulpit and explore the possibilities of a career with Chick-fil-A. Tearfully he told me his story:

Upon his return from a two-week mission project in a distant city, his wife announced that she and their two children were moving back to her hometown. Her

*

Forgetting those things which are behind and reaching forward to those things which are ahead, I press toward the goal for the prize of the upward call of God in Christ Jesus.

Philippians 3:13–14

only reason was that her husband gave too much attention to the church and not enough to his family.

"Had your wife supported your ministry?" I
asked.

"Yes," he said. "She taught Sunday school classes,
often played the piano, came faithfully to worship services with the children. . . . Now I can't step into the
pulpit without looking down at that empty pew. And
when I phone my children, most of my conversation
with my nine-year-old son is unintelligible because we
are both weeping."

We live in a changing world, but the important
things do not change. They never will. The important
things are in abundance, and they are free. Yet how
many take advantage of them?

My daughter Trudy, home from college for the
weekend, told me as we were seated in the family room,
"You know, Dad, the most favorable memories I have of
you are the times when you came to my bedside and
you let me tell you all the things I did during the day."

What? I asked myself. *I don't remember doing that
very often. I thought my daughter would remember our
comfortable home, her fine education we provided, nice
clothes, an automobile . . . .*

Instead, my daughter's fondest memories were of
something that did not cost money. How I wished I
could have turned back the clock. I would provide all
the time my daughter wanted to share with me, especially at bedtime.

Parents should be willing to talk when their children want to talk with them. It is important to listen
with the heart as well as with the ears. When a parent
says, "Let's sit down and talk," children don't have any-

thing much to talk about. It is important to take advantage of unexpected opportunities and talk on *their* schedule.

How good a parent you were is determined by your grandchildren. If I have not taught my children how to be good parents—principally by example—then I have not fulfilled my responsibility. Pray for me and my grandchildren.

After speaking at a church's father-son banquet recently, I was asked by a father who is a psychologist if I would talk to his son who was there by his side.

"I'll wait outside," the father said.

The sixteen-year-old boy told me his father had bought him an automobile, but the father took it away when the son's grades declined.

"My two sisters get straight *A*'s, but passing grades are all I can get," the boy said. "It's embarrassing for me when my friends come over and see my car parked in the driveway."

"Did you and your father have a good relationship before you received the automobile?" I asked.

"Yes, we did," the boy replied.

After chatting awhile, I asked, "Have you ever thought about surrendering the auto to the Lord?"

"What do you mean?"

I said, "You and your dad seldom had a conflict until you received the car, right?"

"Right!"

"Well, if you would be willing to give that car to the Lord, it would no longer be your problem. It would be the Lord's problem, right?"

It took a lengthy conversation to convince the boy that my suggestion was the proper thing to do. "If the car belongs to the Lord," I pointed out, "you won't be disturbed seeing that car parked in the driveway because it's no longer yours.

"One of two things will happen. If you sincerely give it to the Lord, He will enable you to make better grades, or your father will reach some compromises about his requirements. If neither of these two things happens, you're not to worry because it's no longer your problem."

I called the father in and asked his son to explain what he had decided to do. The three of us bowed our heads and prayed that God would intervene in this problem. It was the start of what I hope was a happy outcome of a serious problem threatening the father-son relationship.

Deuteronomy 6:5–7 reminds us to

> love the LORD thy God with all thine heart, and with all thy soul, and with all thy might. And these words, which I command thee this day, shall be in thine heart: And thou shalt teach them diligently unto thy children, and shalt talk of them when thou sittest in thine house, and when thou walkest by the way, and when thou liest down, and when thou risest up (KJV).

In a biblical way, as well as in the practical, instruction is what we say; influence is what we do; and image is what we are.

Instruction is what we say

To be a winner and a leader, a person needs to be very careful about what he says. Sometimes "it's better to remain quiet and be thought a fool than to speak out and remove all doubt."

To be a leader, one needs, of necessity, to communicate with others to relate a message. Lives can be changed if you say the right thing at the right time at the right place with the right spirit. The proper tone of voice and the expression on your face are very important. Body language is also effective—the movement of shoulders, hands, and head is quite noticeable.

Words of encouragement, spoken or written, have a dramatic effect on a person. Likewise, words of correction can be most helpful, but be careful to give them in the proper spirit of helpfulness. Well-intended words, even though they are correct, can damage relationships if they are not perceived as being offered with good will.

One of my team members illustrated these points when his fifteen-year-old daughter came in at 1:30 A.M. He got up from his bed and, with a loud voice, told her to "straighten up or get out."

His daughter responded by getting out. The father then quickly dressed and went out looking for her. But he did not know where to start. Where would a young girl go at 1:30 in the morning?

Influence is what we do

Possibly the greatest power that God has given us is the power of influence. It's still true; our actions speak louder than our words.

As I drove into a service station for some gasoline, an elderly man and a little boy came up. "Would you mind if my grandson put the gas into your auto?" asked the older man.

"Of course not," I replied.

As we stood there watching the grandson work, the grandfather said, "My grandson wants to do everything that I do."

"In a case like that," I replied, "you must be very careful what you do."

As I stated earlier in this book, I encourage young people to associate with the kinds of people they would like to be. I tell them, "If you want to be an *A* student, associate with *A* students. If you want to be a good athlete, associate with good athletes. If you want to be a troublemaker, associate with troublemakers." And then, of course, I add, "If you want to be baldheaded, associate with baldheaded people. If you do not believe this to be factual, observe the hairline of my two sons, now in their thirties. They have been associated with their dad all their lives. Now they, too, are becoming baldheaded."

Through my business, I have observed the great influence Operators have on the young people in their units. This is reflected by the way they answer the telephone, by mannerisms in customer relations, and by their decisions about their vocations. The wife of one Operator noted, "The employees even walk the way my husband walks."

What power we possess, but how often we fail to take advantage of it by not letting our walk match our talk. Give attention to what you do for the sake of others, and it will be good for you as well.

Image is what we are

People generally know us as we are. As Lincoln said, "You may fool all the people some of the time; you can even fool some of the people all of the time; but you can't fool all of the people all of the time." The book of Genesis tells us that we are all created in God's image— in the likeness of God. This puts tremendous responsibility on each of us. It demands our very best in all circumstances, in whatever we undertake to do, so that we might not damage the reputation of our Creator, our heavenly Father. As we often sing, "Love so amazing, so divine, demands my soul, my life, my all."

It is easier to succeed than to fail. Can this be factual? I would like to encourage each reader to discover that the secret to success is no secret at all. It is very obvious, but we are too often blinded to the truth.

Zig Ziglar tells the incredible, but true, story of the Chinese bamboo tree. I looked up the details in the *World Book* and even made a trip to Indonesia to see for myself these fast-growing bamboo trees. The guide I had in Indonesia said you can almost see some of the species of the bamboo tree growing with the naked eye, they grow so rapidly.

The process goes like this: You take a little seed, plant it, water it, and fertilize it for a whole year, and nothing happens. The second year you water it and fertilize it, and nothing happens. The third year you water it and fertilize it, and nothing happens. The fourth year you water it and fertilize it, and nothing happens. How discouraging this becomes! The fifth year you continue to water and fertilize the seed and then . . . take note. Sometime during the fifth year, the Chinese bamboo tree sprouts and grows ninety feet in six weeks!

Life is much akin to the growing process of the Chinese bamboo tree. It is often discouraging. We seemingly do things right, and nothing happens. But for those who do things right and are not discouraged and are persistent, things will begin to happen. Finally we begin to receive the rewards.

We will never reach our greatest potential until we perform at our best. Sometimes it takes only 5 percent more effort to reap 100 percent more dividends.

May I assure you who are kind enough to read this book that it is indeed easier to succeed than to fail, that it takes time to succeed and time to fail, but more time to fail than to succeed. May I encourage you to keep the important things in life *important*. With God's direction, you will eventually receive the rewards that you're seeking and the rewards you deserve.

"May God bless you and keep you and be gracious unto you and give you peace." Amen.

"Truett Cathy's life story presents exactly the type of role model so badly needed in today's fast-paced world. His success inspires anyone who reads his words, because he overcame a lot of odds, and never faltered in his faith.
    J. L. Clendenin
    Chairman of the Board, BellSouth Corporation

"*It's Easier to Succeed Than to Fail* was written from the heart. It is an exciting, dynamic book that will inspire young and old to strive for the very best."
    Eddie J. White
    Principal, Northcutt Elementary School,
    College Park, Georgia

"I loved this book. Truett Cathy is revealed not only as a special man of God with some important lessons to teach us, but as a brilliant storyteller. I read his book on a day my spirits needed a pickup. This book did the job—and then some."
    Tony Campolo
    Professor of Sociology, Eastern College

"*It's Easier to Succeed Than to Fail* will provide the reader with an excellent insight into Truett Cathy's life and work ethic. Truett Cathy is a magnificent individual who personifies the best qualities that humankind possesses, and the reader will be spiritually stimulated and intellectually motivated."
    William M. Suttles
    Acting President, Georgia State University

"[Truett Cathy] outsells everyone else in our food courts in six days while they stay open seven, and this is usually by a wide majority of 30 percent or above the other merchants. . . . he teaches that Christianity, honesty, and hard work will always win. . . . Truett Cathy is one of a kind."
    D. Scott Hudgens
    Scott Hudgens Company